DISCOVER
The SOURCE
Of YOUR
LATENT
ENERGY

SUNDAY ADELAJA

Sunday Adelaja
Discover The Source Of Your Latent Energy
©2017 Sunday Adelaja
ISBN 978-1-908040-81-7

Cover design by Alexander Bondaruk
Interior design by Olena Kotelnykova

TABLE OF CONTENTS

INTRODUCTION

There is a law of conservation of energy: nothing disappears without a trace, and is nothing taken from nowhere. But you can only understand after time, how great the gains and the losses are.

- Sergei Bodrov, Jr. (1971-2002), a Russian film director, actor, screenwriter

Energy is an amazing phenomenon that propels us at every turn. Light, warmth and communication emanate from energy. Our world is impregnated with energy. The world is powered through energy and energy is found in virtually everything, in humans and animals, in trees and in the air, rocks and plants, rivers and lakes, in fossil fuels, energy driven cars, ships, planes, lights and the city lights. The further the advancement in human development, the more the energy that is needed.

Energy is multisided and it possesses multi-dimensional values. The word "energy" is derived from the Greek word that means "action". The scientific world refers to energy as: **"a common quantitative measure of various forms of motion of matter."** During movements of objects (animate or inanimate) energy is released. And energy exists in various forms. For example, when heating anything during a chemical reaction or during decomposition of atoms. The common forms of energy include, kinetic, gravitational, electrical, elastic, chemical, thermal, chemical and radiant energy respectively. All of the many forms of energy are convertible to other kinds of energy.

In the epigraph to the introductory part of the book, 'the law of conservation of energy', Bodrov Jr., states that the Creator has put in all his creations, a certain energy which only changes its shape and **that energy can neither be created nor be destroyed, however, it is converted from one form to another. This means that there is no energy loss in transfer.** Kinetic energy can be converted into heat, then heat to light electrical energy, but the total amount of energy remains unchanged. A practical example of this is in water. When the water boils, it is converted into steam, and when frozen, it turns to ice. During the transition of water from one form to another, the mass of the volume of water remains the same. Likewise, no matter the amount of energy transformation that may occur, the world's energy level remains unchanged. One must understand that there are boundless energy opportunities in the world, and that energy is a "living force".

So, energy is everywhere. We live in a world full of energy, but for some reason, we always lack it, in this book, we will limit our studies to the energy that is in me, in you and in every one of us. We are engaged in the constant search for energy sources, power is needed for all our actions in this world. And because we lack basic understanding on the importance of energy, we are not able to tap into the benefits of energy, we lack insight on how to accumulate and concentrate the force of energy in order to achieve the goals that we set for ourselves.

WHERE IS ENERGY HIDDEN?

The book title is: "Discover Your Source of Latent Energy". Just imagine this, dear reader: "you tapping into the source of stored energy." Where is this latent energy hidden? I want to tell you the great news: the energy we are talking about is already in you! And as we have discussed earlier, according to the law of conservation of energy, energy cannot be created or destroyed, it can only be modified or redirected. This means that, regardless of whether you are using the energy available to you or not, it always exists in the form of potentials in you. The only question is, how will you use it, if you intend to claim it as a required resource. **Energy is always at your disposal, you will always have enough power to do SOMETHING and to do all that you have in mind.**

You may feel inadequate that you lack power and cannot do anything, it is not because you do not have these powers, or that there is no energy. Believe me, you have as much energy in you, as there is in me or any other person! Energy is not an endowment localized to "special peoples". And neither is anyone deprived of power by the Creator. It is confusing for someone to think so. Never say that you lack energy. The amount of energy that God provided and established on this planet has not reduced, it will not be depleted nor will it be added upon. As it was, so will it always be. That is the essence of the law of conservation of Energy. That, energy cannot be created or produced and that it is impossible to destroy, remove or reduce energy. It can only be modified from one state to another. But it already is in us! And it means that you have enough power to accomplish anything you can ever think about or imagine.

Friends, you should know that **if someone does something and SUCCEEDS, achieves outstanding results, it is only possible because he tapped into "available" power in himself**, other people continue to wait for miracles to happen. THE NEEDED ENERGY IS ALREADY WITHIN YOU! We often think that the energy must come to us from outside, but it is already inside us! Energy will not appear supernaturally. You already have all the necessary energy needed to accomplish anything you want to do on the earth. You can only DISCOVER the energy source through knowledge, through research, through the increase in the volume of your personality. That is, your personal involvement and effort is needed for the energy in you to be activated. **It is your personal responsibility to use the energy allotted to you.** But the fact is that you have it and there is no doubt about it you are loaded with energy.

WHERE OUR VITAL ENERGY SHOULD BE DIRECTED?

Do you want to spend the rest of life, selling sugared water or do you want a chance to change the world?

- Steve Jobs

In one way or another, we expend our energy. And the choice is ours, we might decide to spend it on distributing soda at the crossroads of our hometown, or doing something significant with it that could change the whole world. Gaius Julius Caesar (100-44 BC), the Roman statesman and political leader, military leader, and writer looking back at his life's journey, at a certain segment of his life – at 22 years – lamented and exclaimed: "Twenty-two years old, nothing done for immortality!" He was concerned about the legacy he will leave behind after his life is fully spent on the earth. And so, from time to time, he asked himself this question in his lifetime, this question became his motivation and the driving force behind his accomplishments. Dear friends, what is your own motivation, can you ask yourself this question? Or you do not care about how you live your life and about what you spend the energy, generously given to you by the Lord?

Sergei Bodrov, Russian film director, actor and screenwriter, whose words I was quoting at the epigraph, noted that " But you can only understand after time, how great the gains and the losses are." It is possible to discover too late that what we spend our entire life's energy upon what does not have any value, and does not have any bearing on our purpose in life. The energy we have spent is ultimately wasted. What do I mean? One day I came across one amusing inscription on the t-shirt that says, "living a life so that the priest will not have to lie at my funeral." The way we live our lives, determines the kind of story that the priest will tell at our funeral. Our life's story will either reveal the truth about us or the lie we have lived. And this will depend on what we are focusing our energy upon, while we are alive. As long as we walk on this earth having lungs breathing and heart beating, the power is in our hands and we are the architect of our own destiny.

Sooner or later we shall all die, the awesome energy we possess will be left behind. It may either be fully utilized by us or it may remain unused after we have gone. On the other side of destiny, we will not be able to do anything, we cannot change, implement or achieve anything. Can you give any directive to the priest at your funeral, where the energy in your life will be directed? Do you have time before the end of this life to reveal all the potential that is embedded in you? To answer this question, you need to understand where you direct your energy every day of your life. You need to find ways to expand this energy, which is already in you to achieve better results and more. American poet Henry Wadsworth

Longfellow (1807-1882) wrote the following remarkable lines:

Lives of great men all remind us
We can make our lives sublime,
And, departing, leave behind us
Footprints on the sands of time:

It makes sense to only spend the energy of our lives, on achieving greatness, as the poet said, "We can make our lives sublime." The purpose of our lives -. Is to leave an imprint in the history of mankind, to leave our "footprints on the sands of time". I urge you, dear reader, do not settle for anything less. You should not even waste your time! You will save your time, if the time is spent to discover how to tap into our stored energy source, in order to spend it on what is really important in fulfilling our life's purpose. We will be able to gain, not to lose, if we find the answer to this question on time. The intention of this book is to help us do that.

PRACTICAL SUGGESTIONS FOR READING THIS BOOK

This book can change your life!

Often, when reading an inspiring or instructional book, we decide to apply the lessons we have learned. However, sadly, just as often, after only a few weeks, due to the business of life, we slowly forgot about our intentions. The fact is, you can have a lot of diverse and useful knowledge in your head, but if you don't follow through and use it you will never reap the benefits. Much of what you will read here will not be anything new to you, the question is what will you do with what you read here?

Here are six practical steps, that will help empower you to turn your good intentions into good actions:

1. Read this book several times

While reading the truths contained here, pause often to ponder what is being shared. Ask yourself how and when you can practically implement what is recommended in your life. After you have finished a detailed study of the book, re-read it every month as a refresher and a reminder of the truths you have learned. Let this book become a handbook in your tool chest for success.

2. Read out loud

It has been proven that reading out loud helps you to more effectively connect with the truth you are reading, which in turn empowers you to release into your life the power that is contained in every word. It is imperative that you not only see the words, but also that you hear every word. Jesus said, "If anyone has ears to hear, let him hear." And He said to them, "Pay attention to what you hear: with the measure you use, it will be measured to you, and still more will be added to you. For to the one who has, more will be given, and from the one who has not, even what he has will be taken away." (Mark 4:23–25, Emphasis added). Jesus wasn't primarily saying be careful what you hear others say, (though that is vitally important) — what He was emphasizing was the importance of what you hear yourself saying. Why? Because you will believe what you hear yourself saying! Spoken words have a 'wave-like' nature and when they are spoken (and heard), they have a dynamic effect on everything around them. Words are important. Do not neglect the power of Spirit-filled spoken words! Do not let the life-transforming power of your spoken words lay untapped and unused!

3. Underline and take notes

This isn't fiction, it isn't a novel. While reading this book, keep a pen or highlighter nearby. As you read, the truths contained herein will leap out at you. Capture those truths by underlining key words, sentences, and paragraphs. This simple action will significantly increase the impact they will have on you and will enhance your ability to remember them. Also, take the time to record your thoughts and notes in the margins — make this book 'your' book. Underlining not only makes reading the book more interesting, but it also is helpful when you return regularly to review it again.

4. Re-read the underlined portions

As you are impacted by the truths contained here and underline them, it makes it easier to quickly review the most important and personally applicable truths in this book. As I stated earlier, in order to get the best results from reading this book, you should review it often. I encourage you to allow the truths you have marked inspire you to improve your life. I am amazed at our ability, as human beings, with the power we have to remember things. I am just as amazed at our ability to forget. That is why we must do everything we can to help capture the truths we so desperately need so we can both review and apply these truths to our life.

5. Immediately apply the principles learned

The best way to benefit from the truths you will be learning is to consciously apply what you have heard and learned in your life's circumstances. You see, I can teach you, but I can't make you learn. Only you can make that choice. Teaching is a dynamic two-way process. The most effective way to learn is when we put into practice what we have been taught. As you read this book, if you want to master the principles contained here, put them into practice at every opportunity until they are second nature. If you do not practice them, if you do not choose to live them, the sad fact is that you will very quickly forget them. Only that which is recognized as important and of value and put into practice remains in the memory.

6. Set realistic priorities for applying what you learn

Don't try to conquer the whole world at once. You must walk before you run. Instead of trying to do everything you will be learning in this book at once, start by selecting one to three points and begin to apply them in your life until they become second nature. You will only receive the optimal benefit from the truths contained here as you apply them by constant repetition.

At the end of each chapter, you will find golden nuggets which will summarize the most important ideas shared throughout the chapter. To further help cement the truths you will be learning, I have also included self-assessment quizzes designed to help you synergize what you have learned. I have also included practical exercises that will help you implement them and make them an integral part of your lifestyle. They are not designed just for reading. Please read that last sentence again. If you desire to get the maximum results and benefits from these practical exercises, I strongly advise you to start applying them immediately, otherwise, the cares and worries of life will distract you. If you allow that to happen, they will keep you from achieving your destiny and the transformation you desire in your life will not occur.

In my years of sharing these life changing truths with multitudes of people, I have noticed that the difference between those who do and do not succeed, is that those who do succeed do what they know to do. Those who do not succeed usually fail because they do not do what they know to do, or if they do, they do so in a 'superficial' manner.

Life isn't a game — it is for real. It is made up of real choices that have real consequences, for the choices we make. How you approach and engage with the truths in this book; how you study, using the tools provided and how faithfully you apply them to your life's circumstances will be the deciding factor on how much benefit and receive and also how successful you become. Therefore, I ask you to take the exercises seriously, as they are not for the benefit of the author, but rather, because I desire to empower and equip you to succeed. The most effective way to approach the exercises is to get away to a quiet place where you will not be disturbed, perhaps at a time when there is no one else at home, or early in the morning before anyone else is up, or late at night when everyone else is asleep, so you don't have to be concerned about being interrupted.

As you work through the book and the materials, make sure you 'look back' and meditate on the previous chapter(s) and on all the points that you have underlined and highlighted. Reflect on your decisions and write down your follow-up. Don't forget to schedule specific times for your time of study. This will help you stay focused on taking the necessary steps needed to transform your life indefinitely. Share the book and what you have learned with someone else — a study partner — so you have someone to be accountable to, who can partner with you as you work through the book. Write down the date and time you start on your new journey. Let this date be the starting point for a new beginning in your life!

GUIDELINES FOR THE IMPLEMEN-TATION OF PRACTICAL TASKS

1. CAUTION: These tasks are not just to be read; they are VERY IMPORTANT . From my years of sharing these truths with people, I know from experience, how often people 'superficially' perform such tasks. Don't be guilty of making that mistake — this is for you, take them seriously.

2. For optimum results, I suggest you start applying what you learn immediately, otherwise, you run the risk of delaying your success.

3. Find a quiet place and answer all the questions.

4. Meditate on the previous chapter, on everything that you underlined or highlighted, reflect on them and make sure you write out your steps of action.

5. Set yourself a time frame. Do not postpone your new beginnings.

6. Find a study partner — someone to whom you can be accountable to, who can remind you about your goals.

HOW TO TAKE THE SELF-ASSESSMENTS

The self-assessments that follow each chapter are designed to help you check your progress and determine where you are. Recognizing the areas where you need improvement is the first step in knowing where, and how, to apply the principles presented in this book. Respond thoughtfully and honestly to the self-assessments.

For each self-assessment item, there should only be one response. Next to each possible answer you will see a number in brackets denoting the value of that response. Your totaled score will indicate how ready you are to live out the principles in question. The self-assessments are designed only to help you discover your areas that need improvement, not to humiliate you. Remember, we are all a work in progress and we all have areas we can improve in.

If you would like to get some psychological counseling or to participate in our practical training, designed to help facilitate the changes you desire in your life, you can use the following link to register: http://www.universityoflife.com. On this site you will also find many useful resources which will help you to build a successful life. Do not miss out on your opportunity to achieve your destiny!

CHAPTER 1:

THERE IS A LATENT ENERGY IN EVERYONE

Chukchi geologist collected pebbles on the beach. They suddenly saw a hungry polar bear charging towards them. They had no guns. Chukchi had enough skis, and as they started to put them on. A geologist said:

- Useless! Anyway, you cannot run faster than the bear.

- And I, however, do not have to run faster than the bear. I have to run faster than you!

A Joke

When you find yourself in the face of danger, all hidden reserves energy of your body, your mind, will be detected. In the face of danger, you grasp, you become conscious that you are either going to survive at the cost of enormous effort, or find yourself in the clutches of a wild beast, as in the geologists' joke above. So, dear reader, in this chapter I want to talk about the latent energy in you. Why is it "latent"? Because it is existing in the human as

21

potential: it cannot be noticed until the person makes efforts to discover it. The energy is stored but not actively used, "hidden" until better times as potential.

The head physician of one village hospital told me that he nearly got a heart attack after one incident. His maternity ward in the village was not available, and a woman in labor, was sent to the city. On the way, there was an accident and the whole company fell into the ditch ...

At four o'clock in the morning the three of them became four already with the arrival of a child - the driver with the head bandaged, the midwife with the hand in a sling and a young mom with a child. The midwife had a broken collarbone and therefore was only able to give advises. The woman, apparently under great of stress, gave birth, bandaged her attendants, and they all walked together through the night, seven kilometers through the woods on foot. [1]

To help you better understand the situation, I would say that childbirth, is a difficult test for the female organism. Imagine that you both had broken 27 bones! And besides the fact that the woman had the fate of giving birth in extreme conditions, she had been compelled by the situation to provide assistance to victims of car accident and then walk with them, on foot in the night through the forest for seven kilometers. Who would have thought that the one that needs help, will accomplish such feat!

But surely you've heard a lot of cases of incredible strength and energy in extreme conditions. For example, the mother of a child hit by car, was able to lift multi-ton vehicle, just to free up her child from under the wheels of the truck. People, as we read in the anecdote above, developed incredible speed and overcame obstacles that seem insurmountable under abnormal conditions, when they are at risk, for example, broken loose bulldog. LATENT ENERGY IS DORMANT IN US FOR THE TIME BEING, IT DOES NOT MEAN IT DOES NOT EXIST. We need only the right conditions for it to manifest.

But it does not necessarily require extreme circumstances for the energy hidden in us, to manifest. An example of action of the energy inherent in us is what occurs during the growth of hair on our head: after a week or a month is necessary to cut the hair again, because it has "overgrown". Or, what makes a tiny sperm cell of the father fuse with the egg of the mother, though both are invisible to the naked eye, the cells grow and evolve within 9 months, then trigger childbirth and cause a child to be born with the weight of 3 kg? This action is as a result of latent energy. But even at this, the child's growth does not stop, it continues until they reach sexual maturity age. Just imagine it, a defenseless baby, completely dependent on its parent, grows to a six-foot giant, weighing about 90, or even 100 kilograms. All this is possible because of the latent energy that is inherent in the child and works in all areas of growth and development (growth of muscles, bones, organs etc.) Therefore, the latent energy is in all of us and in all spheres of our lives.

WHERE DO PEOPLE WITH DISABILI-TIES DRAW THEIR ENERGY FROM?

I decided to reset the counter of my life and set the arrow to the "Harmony". You can do the same if you want. Let's take a break, think about where we are, where we want to go, how to become the person that will be remembered for the fact that he changed the world for the better and leave his mark

- **Nick Vujicic (1982 p.),**
  Motivational speaker

We quite often have the habit of exaggerating our problems. For some, someone might have a good excuse why he could not do something: "How can I do this? I do not have the power! ". While someone else, perhaps, would have been glad to do something important and significant, but he imagines that his situation is impossible. We often have different excuses, 'we cannot afford it', 'we cannot cope with it'. But there is plenty of evidence in the stories of people living among us who were caught up in the worst situation than we are, they continue to live, and do not give up. Losing hands, people are beginning to use their feet to draw brilliant pictures. Some losing vision or hearing, compensate the other skills and abilities that, in spite of everything, allow them, in the words of Nick Vujicic, BECOME PEOPLE WHO CHANGE THIS WORLD FOR THE BETTER AND LEFT THEIR MARK.

In the phrase "helpless situation", a person whom the hand does not obey feet – is helpless? If we consider at the same time, and if he thus successfully works, studies in a foreign university, won the Olympics Games, which was organized by international IT-company? There is nothing quicker than thought.

When the training centre of IBA corporation held in Belarus the Olympic Games on bases of system administration among people with limited possibilities. Completely paralyzed inhabitant of Borisov, Alexander Makarchuk, completed the task first. Having come off the second result for 40 minutes. The interesting thing is that he controls the cursor using his voice.

Alexander lost the mobility of the arms and legs due to illness at the age of 17 years. Despite this, he finished school and studied at the department of civil law and procedure in the Russian interregional social institution. In jurisprudence young man saw an opportunity to look for a job in the Russian labor market, because this profession is suitable for disabled: with the use and of voice only, he could advise customers on Skype.

He was considered for the position of System Administrator. In that same competition the IBA, which we discussed above, Alexander won a certificate for a free training and the opportunity to pass the international certification for system administration. This international certificate will allow him to work remotely as an administrator in any country of the world. A few years ago he created the site "Unlimited" - which is intended for those who, like him, are in a "helpless" state. Alexander fills his website with information for this very purpose : to demonstrate that despite the limitations, you can help yourself or your loved one. "BY HELPING YOURSELF, YOU PAVE THE WAY FOR OTHERS", - said the young man.

Where did this artist draw her energy from, after losing her sight? *A graduate of the British School of Arts 29-year-old Claire Lawrence from Siston; her creativity encouraged other artists to continue not to allow disability be what will prevent them in following their dreams. Claire was diagnosed with Autosomal Retinitis Pigmentosa, a degenerative eye condition, though when she was eight years old she had almost a normal vision, however in her University years she was registered Blind. In her own words she wrote "Despite my increasingly deteriorating vision I chose to go ahead with my art degree; this was my passion and I wanted to do it while I could still see. My work both then and now tends to focus on the tactile; I like to push materials to their limits; freezing, burning, deconstructing and rebuilding. I enjoyed spectacle in art and want the viewer to experience and enjoy my work at different levels.*

Following the completion of my degree in 2007 my eyesight took a sharp decline. I had given up on creating art work, I couldn't see the point, excuse the pun. However, in 2013, with my eyesight as stable as it had been for 3 years, and frustration at my lack of creativity peaking, a moment of inspiration, the gift of a blow touch and desire to express myself kick-started and revived my creative passion." [3]

The artist used the frozen and burned materials, recycling of raw products. The pieces in the series of her painting called "autosomal" were created by burning, stitching, vanishing and layering canvas. This created an intricate depth of paintings. The burnt hole in the painting according to Claire, represented the disintegration of her retina and the way she viewed the world. Her paintings and art works are the expression of her desire to support the blind and visually impaired artists, and as a result of her creativity, she could urge them not to give up. The British believed that a truly creative person always finds a way to express himself [3]. Oddly enough, Claire Lawrence disease has given a new impetus to her work and gave her the strength, energy and inspiration to do what she is doing now.

Where does he derive the energy from, a man whose hands and feet are missing? Yes, we are all familiar to Nick Vujicic, motivational speaker, whose words I have used as an epigraph. Despite his physical limitations, he swims, types fast on a computer and does a lot of other incredible things.

Although Nick Vujicic was born with tetra-amelia syndrome - a rare hereditary disease, which leads to the absence of the four limbs, he is completely independent and lives a full and rich life: he got two degrees, he types letters at a computer speed of 43 words per minute, he surfs, he is fond of fishing, he swims, and he even dives in the pool and rivers. His life is a perfect example of how to overcome the difficulties, the frustrations and limitation, as a result of the faith he had in himself against all odds. Nick Vujicic speaks with openness about his phys-

ical limitations and life's experiences, about how it was not easy to come to terms with his condition. In his life, there was even a time when he wanted to commit suicide. Nick took many years to learn how to see problems as growth opportunity, not an obstacle, on how to set big goals and always achieve the desired objectives.

Nick has traveled to more than 45 countries, speaking in schools, universities and other organizations. He participates in the TV show and writes books. In 2005, Nick Vujicic was nominated for the "Young Australian of the Year". In 2009, he participated in the shooting of the movie "Butterfly Circus", the storyline is about a man without limbs, his will and his faith. In February 12, 2012 held a wedding ceremony Vujicic Nick and Kanae Miyahara, and February 14, 2013 they had a son - Kiyoshi James Vujicic [4].

Nick Vujicic wrote the book **"Life Without Limits: Inspiration for a Ridiculously Good Life"** In it, he formulated the rules of life, which helped him find a way out of difficult life circumstances. " Your life is your own novel. Start writing its first chapter right now! Fill your book with adventure, love and happiness. Live the story, you designed for yourself "[5]. This is a message from a man without arms and legs full of energy and optimism. Rather than being the one that drew his strength in others, Nick Vujicic became for many a source of inspiration and self-confidence. Looking at it, other people gain new energy for their future life without excuses upon excuses.

Remember the words that I quoted at the beginning: "I decided to reset the counter of my life and set the arrow to the" Harmony ". Expanding his latent energy, Nick works from the inside out, from what he feels within and not from adverse life circumstances. He finds the strength not only to continue to live, but to live productively and unselfishly. He calls each of us to do what he did in his life, think about where we are and where we want to be. This legless and armless person considered the most important goal in his life is to live to **"become a man that will be remembered for the fact that he changed the world for the better and LEAVE HIS MARK."** Shouldn't this be the goal of each one of us?

THE STORY OF A BLIND PILOT

"You can get to world-class, you can make excuses, you can't do both"

- Robin Sharma (6 JULY, 2015) Canadian writer, one of the best known in North America for motivating professionals, leadership and personal development

I just need to share with you the life story of one man who, despite the fact that he had lost sight, he climbed the mountains, he swims and dives, he crossed the desert, and did many other things in his eventful life! He discovered his latent energy, and performed some spectacular feats that, even quite healthy people consider impossible. Miles Hilton-Barber is a unique personality and a tireless adventurer.

He was born December 20, 1948 in Harare, Zimbabwe. An ordinary boy. As a teenager, he decided to follow in the footsteps of his father - to become a pilot. Having reached the age of eighteen, Miles went to the flight school, but failed his medical examination because of his sight. He received the terrible news that in three years: due to a genetic predisposition, he will soon go blind. This eventually happened. For thirty years, Miles lost his sight completely. Becoming blind, he moved to England and worked at the Royal National Institute for the Blind. Remembering those times, the blind pilot Miles Hilton-Barber said: "I was afraid to walk 400 meters to the nearest supermarket for a loaf of bread."

What led to such a spectacular change in the life of this man? He was motivated by his younger brother Jeff. It so happened that he was also blind, but that did not stop Jeff in accomplishing his goals. Jeff wanted to go on a single voyage on his yacht from Africa to Australia. And he did it! Jeff's example forced his older brother to change the attitude towards blindness, it inspired him to carry out on his own dream. This led to the world record of achievements for Miles. In 1998 he took part in the London Marathon, and in 1999 has overcome one of the toughest marathons across the Sahara Desert. In 2000, he climbed to the top of Mount Kilimanjaro. During his life he was able to make a flight in a balloon through Nevada on a light airplane flight across the English Channel and ride in a sleigh on Antarctica to the South Pole. In 2002, he was part of a team of three people with disabilities, whose purpose was to travel around the world with more than eighty types of transport. In 2003, he became the first blind pilot who flew over the English Channel on a passenger plane.

During all this time, Miles Hilton-Barber become an incredibly popular figure. Today, he is a highly sort out motivational coach. In the last couple of years, he gave lectures in more than 60 countries. His audience, he talks a lot about his fate, about how he was completely crushed and broken by his disability. He says that he was angry about it and he was offended by the whole world for what happened to him in his early years, when he lost his sight. Miles also said that the only hope he had, have been in God and the doctors who gave him strength to continue to live, but rather than just, simply to exist. As years goes by, Miles realized that it is a waste of time bellyaching about things that cannot be changed in his life, and because he had lost the most precious thing that is common in every human being – which is, time. And then he decided to break the framework of his life - did not wait with hope for change that must come from the outside, and he began to use his latent energy, and thereby became the architect of his own life.

This unique man was sure that everyone is master of his own destiny, and that there are no restrictions in the world that will be able to stop us from achieving our objectives, of course, except those we invent and build for ourselves. "THE ONLY THING HOLDING ME BACK WAS FIVE INCHES, THE DISTANCE BETWEEN MY EARS". And these five centimeters is able to deprive us of the most precious things in life: power, strength, inspiration and optimism. He began his journey to his dream, when he was already 50 years old, but even at that time he managed to achieve incredible results! This man is full of vitality, full of enthusiasm. And what about the energy and optimism you have with you, dear reader, what are you doing with it? That is a billion dollar question you will have to answer for yourself.

Miles Hilton-Barber made this amazing powerful statements

- «Listen! Stepping out of your circle, attempting new things, is the way to broaden and enrich your life, to achieve your dreams!"

- "It is simply amazing how much you can achieve by just keeping going, as long as you are pointing in the right direction!"

- «Your disability should not feature in your goals or dreams when talking about looking at what you want to achieve '"

- "I'm living a dream," he said, "And hoping to enable other blind people in the world to have their dream fulfilled of getting their sight back again."

- Your quality of life, as I keep on telling you, is determined, not so much by your circumstances, but by your response to them! Remember... Dream, decide, plan, persevere.... [6]

Example Miles Hilton-Barber's proves to us that, regardless of our circumstances in life, problems and lack of resources, we always have enough inner life energy to transform us for the better, not only our self, but the whole world around us. Despite the fact that this man could justify his inaction and impotence to quite understandable reasons, he wasn't looking for excuses. At the point he took the first step, Miles Hilton-Barber chose the dream that lives in his heart, against his disability, - blindness.

Robin Sharma, whose words I quoted as an epigraph to the last section of this chapter, confirms how important this choice: "You can get to world-class, you can make excuses, you can't do both". When we are looking for excuses, then we deprive ourselves of the power to change something, overlapping the last source of energy that is necessary for us to take life into our own hands. But the desire to accumulate the results in our energy, allows us a fully armed approach to solving any problems and difficulties which we might have encountered in life. Our life is given to us for great things. And as in all, there is a hidden energy we need, to live a full life, constantly and relentlessly moving toward the goal we have set ourselves, reaching new peaks of life!

So, dear reader, we have come to the end of the first chapter of the book entitled "DISCOVER THE SOURCE OF LATENT ENERGY". In this chapter, you learned that the latent energy is easily detected in extreme circumstances. We reviewed the example of how some seemly hopelessly ill people or people with disabilities derive their energy. We found out that their adverse condition was not a sentence or an excuse for them not live a full life, a life dedicated to the fulfillment of dreams and internal disclosure of gifts and potential. In the next chapter, dear reader, we are going for a crash course on the theory of physical phenomena that explain the nature of the Law of conservation of energy, which is the basis for our discussion in this book.

THE GOLDEN NUGGETS

- Latent energy is "hidden" Because it is existing in the human as potential: it cannot be noticed until the person put pressure to it. The energy is stored but not actively used, "hidden" from time to time as potential

- Latent energy is dormant in us, but that does not mean that it is not there.

- Learn to see problems as a growth opportunity, to set big goals and always achieve the desired outcome, and not an obstacle

- Through our own example, we can change the attitude of other people to their problems and disadvantages, in so doing, we encourage them to pursue their dreams

- People with disabilities derive their energy among difficult circumstances and share it with the people around them

- «Fill your book (life) with adventures, love and happiness. Live the story, which is designed for you. " (Nick Vujicic)

- Live life to the fullest, consistently and relentlessly moving forward toward the goal you set, reaching new peaks of life!

SELF-EXAMINATION TEST

It should be noted only one answer is required for each question or statement. Next to each answer are marked point. Stacked score will determine the outcome of your training.

1. How are the days of your life?

a. My days are beyond me. Sometimes am happy and having fun with friends, some other times am angry and hate others. I always feel tired and depressed. It's like my life is drifting away, and I can hardly remember the last day. Sometimes I even hate life -**1 point**

b. Every day of my life is filled with meaning, fulfilling purpose - that is the main mission of my life. I strive to achieve the goals and dedicate every day of my life to the Creator - **4 points**

c. I live in this world in order to be useful. I care about myself, loved ones, friends. It happens that I can help even a stranger - **3 points**

d. Every day I think only about how to do things that is beneficial to me. I think thoughts that are intended to give me success and happiness - **2 points**

2. Where do you direct the energy of your life?

a. I like to have fun, go out and have fun, be happy to spend all my time in the circle of like-minded people - **1 point**

b. My energy is directed continuously to improve the purpose, to which I am called. I constantly think about how to improve my business. - **4 points**

c. Often direct my energy to take care of relatives and friends, and becoming who I am supposed to be, as a person - **3 points**

d. My energy is directed solely to the make progress, to achieve success in life, that to me what I love, and respected - **2 points**

3. Do you have a dream?

a. Not now, but I remember that in my childhood I had dreams. Life is now hardened for me, my life is all about survival, not about dreams - **2 points**

b. What sort of dream? I even think about it, but do not want. I know that in this life nothing is impossible to achieve, it is only necessary to strive, to earn a piece of bread - **1 point**

c. I have a dream, and I have kept it carefully, and with no one to share, "touch wood". I live in the hope that it will come to pass by itself when the right time comes - **3 points**

d. Of course, I have a dream, and not one. I'm doing everything to ensure that it is accomplished in this life. Even if I cannot wait for its execution, for their part, I am doing everything to make it come true. And it will come true, and will be relevant for people who will live after me - **4 points**

4. What is the dream you have?

a. Nothing. I don't have any dream I currently exist, and am trying to survive. I don't have a clue why I was born into this life. - **1 point**

b. All the childhood dreams I had have disappeared. Now the only thing I think about is achieving success and prosperity - **2 points**

c. I have a dream of happiness for my family and I. For people to fulfill their desire for us to prosper, create beautiful strong family and have kids. - **3 points**

d. I have a dream to create something great for the good of humanity and to realize my full potential. To live a life that is a blessing even to those who will live after me. - **4 points**

5. How much energy are you filled with to achieve your goals and realize your dream?

a. I am filled with energy to realize my dreams and goals, because I know the laws of accumulation and conservation of energy and am practicing them. Also, I'm sure that I have everything planned out, all my dreams will come true, because I do my best to be effective - **4 points**

b. The life energy is there, but it is hardly enough, so I ensure that I only do care about myself - **2 points**

c. What are the objectives? What is energy? There is no strength nor the desire to do something - **1 point**

d. Energy, of course there is, but I'm not sure, that I will do something to get my goals and dreams realized - **3 points.**

TEST RESULTS

From 0 to 7 points - If your total falls within this number of points - it says that you always live in the vital energy shortage. Life goes on as usual, and you are trying to survive in this situation, and trying to stay afloat. You do not expect anything good from life, but you are simply existing, angry at the world more and more. You will need to discover the latent source of vital energy in you and live a fulfilled life! This book you are holding in your hands will help you discover that energy. You will appreciate it so much. You will discover a new, level of strength and fulfilment in life! Good luck and success to you as you go into this adventure to restore your inner man!

From 8 to 16 points - This score indicates that you do not just wonder about the meaning of life, the force that fills the world. You learn to set goals and achieve them. For you, dream of greatness is not something mediocre. But it seems difficult for you to realize your dream. You have the potential to fulfill your destiny. You learned not to give up and strive for realization. What's stopping you - is the concentration on yourself and loved ones. You need to think bigger and to devote time each day fulfillment of your purpose. Good luck in solving the internal vital energy!

From 16 to 20 points – The score here tells a lot about your strength and energy. You never stop, you know your vital energy and you qualitatively distribute it in the right direction. For you, nothing can stop you for achieving your goals. You clearly see the end result and strive every day to make every effort to implement the projects for the benefit of mankind. You are not bustled with activities, and every time you achieve the goals you set for yourself. Good luck, success and good results!

PRACTICAL TASKS

1. Due to the fact that latent energy is in everything, why can't you achieve better results? Think about what did not allow you to realize your potential. Make a list of your goals in life. Record 5 points for each goal that will lead to the implementation and achievement of these goals.

2. What did you learn from the story of people with disabilities mentioned in this book? What are the lessons you can learn from the life of Nick Vujicic and Miles Hilton-Barber?

CHAPTER 2:

THE CYCLE OF ENERGY TRANSFORMATION

Well, dear reader, let's continue our journey into the world of hidden energy. In the last chapter we found out that latent energy manifests itself in situations that require human exertion of all his moral, physical, and spiritual vitality. For example, people with disabilities, we have seen a stunning example of how they unleashed the stored energy source. In this chapter, dear reader, we will talk about a continuous cycle of transformation (conversion) of energy.

Thus, energy - the universal value for the description of physical phenomena.

Energy can be defined as the strength and vitality that is required for a sustained physical or mental activity. Energy can be transferred from one body to another. It can also undergo changes (that is, transformed) from one form to another. The law of conservation of energy is a fundamental law of nature, established empirically, that is experienced by all. It is the physical quantity which will be maintained over time and may be introduced for the isolated physical system. This value is called the energy, and is a scale (from the Latin scalaris -. Step), i.e., the size of each value that can be expressed in a real number. That energy is a function of system parameters.

This law states that ENERGY CAN NOT DISAPPEAR OR APPEAR FROM NOTHING: **in a closed system, i.e. a system that is isolated from its surroundings, the total energy of the system is conserved.** The law states that nature does not allow for the emergence of energy from nowhere and then disappears it into nowhere. There are only two possibilities: in exactly the same size, in which one body loses energy, and another body assimilates it; as much there is a decrease of one type of energy the same energy is added to another species. The law of conservation of energy does not refer to specific events and values, and reflects a general pattern that can be applied everywhere and always, it is sometimes called the law of physics, and the principle of conservation of energy.

The law of conservation of energy is universal, which means it can be equally inherent in systems of diverse physical nature, and from a fundamental point of view of the energy conservation, the law is a consequence of the homogeneity of time, that is, the independence of the laws of physics by the time at which the system is considered. Implementation of energy conservation law in each specific system is subject to its own specific laws of dynamics and are different for different systems.

Historically, in various branches of physics, the law of conservation of energy was formulated independently in connection with, which, different types of energy were introduced. But in any case we speak about the transition of energy from one type to another, despite the fact that the total energy of the system is maintained and in the amount of certain types of energy. In view of the energy division is conditional on various kinds, such a division cannot always be made clear. [7]

For each type of energy conservation law can have a formulation that is different from the universal formulation. For example, in classical mechanics, there is a law of conservation of mechanical energy in thermodynamics - the first law of thermodynamics, and electrodynamics - Poynting theorem *"The principle of the conservation of mechanical energy states that the total mechanical energy in a system (i.e., the sum of the potential plus kinetic energies) remains constant as long as the only forces acting are conservative forces."*

The first law of thermodynamics, in the formulation of its discoverers H. Mayer and Helmholtz says that with all the changes taking place in an isolated system, the total energy of the system remains constant. Another formulation of this reads as follows: energy cannot be created nor destroyed (not destroyed) for all macroscopic physical and chemical processes, but are only converted from one form to another.

The law of conservation of energy applies to the processes occurring in living organisms. **It is found that the total amount of energy that is used by plant, animal or person for a certain period of time, subsequently found again in three types:**

- Plants get their food directly from Sun by using the light Energy of Sun to make food.

- Animals receive energy from the food they eat;

- Living organisms acquire energy the need for life through various metabolic pathways (photosynthesis and cellular respiration) [8]

WHAT DOES PHOTO-SYNTHESIS TELL US?

It is a process by which, in the final instance, depend on all aspects of life on our planet.

-   Timiryazev   (1843-1920), Russian scientist, physiologist

"From the law of conservation of energy we can make a conclusion that energy cannot come out of nothing and disappear without a trace, it is only transformed from one form to another. Energy cannot be created or destroyed, it can only be modified or redirected. In the natural sciences it is a clearly defined phenomenon. It is found that the total amount of energy produced by plants, animals or man for some period of time thereafter is detected again in the emitted heat, the outer, or external materials. THIS MEANS THAT THE PROCESS OF TRANSFORMATION OF ENERGY IS CONTINUOUS.

Especially clearly seen is the example of photosynthesis. It is known that from plants begin almost all food chains. They convert the energy of sunlight into energy nutrient placed in carbohydrates, which is the most important - six-carbon sugar (glucose). This energy conversion process is called photosynthesis. Other organisms have access to this energy by eating the plants. So are food chains that support the planetary ecosystem.

The history of the study of photosynthesis associated with the name of the English philosopher and amateur naturalist Joseph Priestley (1733-

1804), who in 1771 discovered that plants can "fix" the properties of air, "contaminated" as a result of burning or animal waste. Scientists have shown that in the presence of plants, previously contaminated air was purified. To do this in a closed vessel, put under the light, a mouse was place in the vessel with green plant. Due to oxygen released by photosynthesis, the mouse continued to exist for a long time. In the absence of any light and any plants, the mouse quickly choked. Thus, Priestley proved that the light plant absorbs carbon dioxide and produces oxygen. Because carbon dioxide and water plants synthesize organic matter. This process was called photosynthesis.

Robert Mayer, who discovered the law of conservation of energy, in 1845, suggested that plants convert the energy of sunlight into the energy of chemical compounds produced during photosynthesis. According to him, "propagated in space sunbeams" captured "and stored for later use as needed." Later, the Russian Scientist K. Timiryazev proved chlorophyll molecules that are part of the green leaves, and they played the most important role in the plants in the use of sunlight energy. Formed during photosynthesis, carbohydrates (sugars), are used as an energy source and building blocks for the synthesis of various organic compounds in plants and animals. In higher plants photosynthetic processes occur in chloroplasts - the specialized organelles of the plant cell energy conversion [9].

The role of the process of photosynthesis is so hard to overestimate. What Timiryazev called this process "by which, in the final instance, depended on all aspects of life on our planet." And it is quite reasonable, as photosynthesis - is the main supplier of not only organic compounds, but also free oxygen on Earth. Photosynthesis produced in the world an approximately 150 Bln. Tonnes of organic matter, and about 200 Bln. Tonnes per year of free oxygen, while the green plant leaf uses only 1-2% of the energy of the incident light. Isn't this amazing?

The overall equation of photosynthesis is: carbon dioxide + water + light = carbohydrates and oxygen. Thus, the air that we breathe through photosynthesis is saturated with oxygen. But at the same time, carbon dioxide, which we breathe out is absorbed by plants, then the plants again release oxygen, which is necessary for us to breathe. Here's a cycle of energy! Do you see here the closed loop? That energy is not taken out of nowhere: the plant independently, for animals or humans - independently. Everything is already there on the ground! The fact is that when plant "breathe" it gives us oxygen, and when we breathe, it is "carbon dioxide" to plants as oxygen is to us: i.e., food and life. Here is a symbiosis of plants and animals, here's a continuous cycle of energy: **that energy does not disappear and does not appear out of nowhere, it is converted (transformed) from one form to another!**

What conclusions can you draw from these facts for yourself? The above principle applies not only to photosynthesis, it **works always and everywhere, particularly in the life of each of us. This principle says that all the energy we need to be all that we want to be, is already within us, all the energy available for us on earth!**

Therefore, WE SHOULD NOT LOOK FOR STRENGTH OR ENERGY ELSEWHERE, IT IS ALREADY IN US, WE JUST HAVE TO KNOW HOW TO ACTIVATE IT. We can use all the power in us to be a genius, but it all depends on our understanding of this principle. That is, we can reach every vertex, we wish in life. We need to remember that we can transform the energy of the same quality into a completely different quality of energy - activate it. But there is one little "but", **and this but is: - the only way to the top, to which we are aspiring, is only possible through work and through knowledge.**

HOW TO DISCOVER OUR LATENT ENERGY THROUGH WORK?

Some people want it to happen, some wish it would happen, and others make it happen.

- Michael Jordan (1963 p.), The famous American basketball player and former NBA player

What needs work? **Almost all the rich people started their ascent to the top from the state of poverty.** AND THEY BECAME RICH DUE TO THE FACT THAT THEY, BY THE DYNAMISM OF BRAINWORK, WERE ABLE TO CONVERT THEIR ENERGY INTO GOODS AND PRODUCTS THAT ARE IN GREAT CONSUMER DEMAND, allowing them to further improve their material and financial status. We all know the name of Henry Ford. But few people think about how this man was able to reach such heights: to become the "father" of the automotive industry, the first to organize the assembly-line technique of car production, and thus having the opportunity to start production of cars on an industrial scale. *By the early 1920s, he received the title of "King of cars" since he sold more cars than all his competitors combined. At that time, 7 out of 10 purchased cars in the US, were production of Henry Ford. He owned factories, mines, coal mines – all that was necessary for the production of cars, thus creating, his own empire in auto manufacturing. Until now, he created the company operation, being the 4th in volume car production in the world [10].* Henry Ford died a long time ago, but the idea, which his vision gave birth to and materialized in the visible physical world, continues to live, producing more and more new products which are relevant. *The legendary businessman twentieth century Henry Ford was born in 1863 on a farm near the provincial town Dearborn, in the northwest of the US state of Michigan. Henry's parents did not approve of his passion for mechanics, which began when he was 12-year-old, the first time he saw a car that made a great impression on him. From that moment the boy did not leave the dream to construct the moving mechanism. His father and mother wanted to see their son become "respectable farmer," so, when Henry at age 17 became an apprentice in a machine shop, this news was for them was almost a tragedy. [10]* Ford was obsessed with the idea to create a car that is available to everyone: his dream is, to turn the millions of ordinary pedestrians to be proud owners of cars. But he was not content with the fact that he nurtured the idea at the level of dreams. He believed that "the ideas themselves are valuable, but every idea, after all, is just an idea. The challenge is **"to implement it in practice."** Therefore, he did not just have the dream, and he made a titanic effort aimed at ensuring that his dreams became a reality. *But towards the realization of a dream we do not always become successful. Similarly, the same thing happened with Ford: he constructed in his spare time, his first car, he searched for his potential customers, but encountered only mocking inhabitants. His first invention was not in demand. However, Ford was not discouraged and he continued to fight for his dream, showing persistence and perseverance. Whatever happens, he stubbornly told himself:* ***"When it seems that the whole world is against you, remember that the airplane always takes off against the wind!" [10].***

The customer base for Ford began to grow. This helped him to attract investors and to set up his own company - Ford Motor Company. All the efforts of the young company were directed on the creation of a universal car: a simple, reliable and cheap as initially conceived by Ford. While the idea of a "car for everybody" was a novelty to many, mass car was something fantastic. Like now, for example, we would have reacted to the idea of "the mass of the aircraft?" However, Henry continued to be faithful to the dream, he was not distracted by extraneous or secondary purpose and was not baffled by the opinions of others. He continued using hard work to translate his ideas and dreams into the real physical world. As a result of hard work, Ford became a pioneer in the automotive industry, and a wealthy man.

Ford simplified the design of the car, by standardizing its parts and mechanisms. He was the first in the world to begin the use of conveyor for the production of machines, and this innovative solution in the blink of an eye pivoted the company to become the leader in car industry, leaving the competition far behind. Yes, the conveyor was used in the XIX century, but Henry Ford with its help, he realized his dream and achieved unprecedented success. The mass production of model "Ford T", whose sales brought huge profits was established in 1908. By 1914, Ford had produced about 10-million cars of the famous brand. While 10% of all cars in the world were these machines [10].

Henry Ford, in fact embodied the "American Dream" into reality, realized his mission to improve people's lives. Henry Ford values can be clearly understood by this statement, **"The only true test of values, either of men or of things, is that of their ability to make the world a better place in which to live"** [10]. Henry Ford became the man who through work could reveal the hidden power in him. His financial success was due to the fact that he was able to convert his energy and achieve the realization of his dreams - in particular car, by offering humanity an affordable means of transportation.

Michael Jordan has identified three categories of people: **"Some people want it to happen, some wish it would happen, and others make it happen."** That is, for something to happen in my life, it is not enough to desire it or dream about it. For my dream to become a reality

I need to take action and work to - convert energy into something visible, that is, working to convert the energy into physical tangible product. A striking example of a person who to converted his energy to material reality, thereby, making his dreams come true, is Henry Ford.

RECIPE FOR EFFICIENCY

When I work fourteen hours a day and seven days a week, I get lucky

— Armand. Hammer

If you are working consistently, and you are able to transform your energy in your chosen direction, then sooner or later you will undoubtedly succeed, your efficiency, your effectiveness will increase! This is confirmed by numerous facts from the life of famous people:

- The mathematician **Paul Erdos** last 25 years of his life devoted 19 hours a day pursuits of higher mathematics.
- The inventor in the field of electrical engineering and radio engineering, engineer, physicist **Nikola Tesla** was a great scientist, ahead of his time. He could hardly sleep and thus his productivity was outstanding. He began his day at three in the morning and worked until 11 pm seven days a week. The strength of his concentration can be seen in one of his sayings: "I'm absolutely exhausted, but I cannot stop working. My experiments are so important, so beautiful, so amazing that I can hardly tear myself away

from them to eat. And when I try to sleep, all the time I am thinking about them. "

- The writer **Honore de Balzac** was able to work 15 hours a day; thanks to this, he was able to publish three to six books a year. And, if you remember, it was not the age of the Internet and high-tech, where you utilize computer and other tools to facilitate the writing of any literary work. At that time, he wrote by hand using pen and candle light - because electricity was not there then.

- Another, no less than a great man, a German composer Johann **Sebastian Bach**, after his death, left a musical heritage of this size that only the meeting and the publication of his works took 46 years. If you had to hire one person for an 8-hour working day for all the works of Bach to be reproduced, then it will take about 70 years!

- The ingenious artist and inventor **Leonardo da Vinci's** slept for 15-20 minutes a day every 4 hours (a total of about 2 hours), the remaining 22 hours Leonardo worked.

- American entrepreneur **John D. Rockefeller,** before becoming the most dollar millionaire in the history of mankind, had to help his family, being the eldest child, get out of poverty. Worked as self-employed. His health was an envy: on the threshold of the office, John always appeared at 6.30 am and came out of it only at 10 pm.

- The operation of the extremely prolific artist, **Salvador Dali**, hit others. Very often, closing in his room and working furiously, he forgot to go down to the dining room. In his youth, despite his talent, Salvador Dali every day attended the Academy of Arts and learned to paint there until exhaustion.

- **Mark Zuckerberg**, founder of Facebook, says that "the real story behind Facebook - is that we all worked very hard. Enough boring story, is not it? We just sat there for six years and wrote computer code. " In addition to high performance, Zuckerberg showed a high concentration and focus on the task at hand: "I spend almost all my time on Facebook. I have almost no time for new hobbies. So I set myself clear objectives. "

We can make conclusions for ourselves - **in order to become successful in life, we must:**

- Detect the source of hidden energy.
- Start to release it through hard work.
- Direct energy in the right direction, so that at the appointed time we get the expected result.

The name Bill Gates is now known to almost everyone on the planet Earth. Everyone knows that a small computer company Microsoft he managed to turn into a software giant manufacturer. It is known that a brilliant young mathematician quit Harvard University in order to establish his own company. Why did he refuse to go through beaten path, against the wishes of parents who wanted to see their son become a lawyer? What prompted him to violate generally accepted standards and rules, and to plunge into the risky world of business?

His passion was computer programming, which hooked him since childhood. By providing parents, he was able to study in a private school for the children of the elite, "Lakeside". There he became acquainted with the computer. His parents did not regret the three thousand dollars spent for the purchase of a computer terminal, which was a rarity even in the majority of colleges in 1968. In addition, it was an advanced device for that time, so that Bill and his comrades did not have to learn programming using the labor-intensive systems, which at that time enjoyed almost everything. With the help of the school parents' committee they established the so-called Teletype ASR-33 - terminal operating in a time-sharing and directly linked to a computer in downtown Seattle. [11]

Thus, Bill Gates got the unique opportunity to learn programming in real time in the eighth grade. It was to his great advantage. But not only did his wealthy and generous parents played a crucial role in the fate of the Bill, but also, if not for his personal efforts, no one would have ever found out the name of this young man. His parents did what they could, as it relates to their own part, but Bill Gates had focused all his energy on the most important thing for himself. After spending a lot of time on a painstaking work, he eventually superseded everyone.

A new company had opened in Seattle called Computer Center Corporation. It had a mainframe computer. The boys nicknamed the company

C-Cubed for the three Cs in its name. Few people understood computers then. So C-Cubed turned to the bright boys at Lakeside School and made a deal. The boys could use the company's mainframe computer for free if they would help the company search out for "bugs," or flaws, in their programs. For Bill and his friends, this job was paradise. Here was a huge computer worth millions of dollar, under their control.

As he recalls, Bill Gates, he was obsessed with computers, spending time in the computer lab until late at night. Then his friend found a free computer time in the University of Washington, the free time interval was from three in the morning to six in the morning. Therefore, Gates will leave the house at night and walked to the university to take advantage of this opportunity. Do you think such a passion and an obsession with things you love, will not bring results? However, Bill's mother did not know about it, and because she could not understand why her son was so hard to get in the morning ... [11]. Bill Gates used all the opportunities that came his way. If he had, it is unlikely that was not as agile and nimble to reach those heights, which is now known to all. Any success is worth something, and Gates paid a price. He did not come down to the summit of success by helicopter, bypassing all the difficult thorny paths. He is not driven at someone else's expense. He worked very hard, and that success that smiled at him, was just reward for a titanic and selfless work. *Another such "happy" chance was the opportunity to do his favorite thing in the framework of the research project with a technology company, which has established a computer system on a huge power station on the south of the State of Washington. Having persuaded the school teachers, and to take time off from classes, Bill spent all spring to work under the direction of John Norton, who, according to Gates, taught him about the programming like no one ever did. [11]* What could be better than to start his career, studying with the acclaimed master in his business? Is this not being the next step to the success of Bill Gates?

While still very young, Bill Gates had transformed his energy in one direction. He considered all secondary ambitions as superfluous - teaching at Harvard had fallen victim to such an approach - rushing for only one purpose: to realize his dream, his potential: that is, to reveal his latent energy.

So we started this chapter with you, dear reader, with a majestic picture of the continuous cycle of transformation (conversion) energy. you will remember what photosynthesis is and the sound of the law of conservation of energy. Do not disregard this information, as it is important, it will help us to further our discussions throughout the book. In the next chapter you will find a discussion of how to make best use of the reproductive energy in your life. You will learn what is the true purpose of the reproductive energy.

THE GOLDEN NUGGETS

- Energy cannot come out of nothing and disappear without a trace, it is only converted from one form to another
- The process of energy transformation is a continuous one.
- There is a continuous cycle of energy in nature: the fact is that what the plant "breath" becomes oxygen for us, and what we breathe out, becomes "carbon dioxide" for them
- All the energy we need to be everything we want to be, is already in us, all the energy available to us
- We do not need to search for strength or energy, it is already within us, we just have to be able to activate it.
- The path to the height of anything we aspire to reach, is through work and through knowledge
- Almost all the rich people started their ascent to the height in life in state of poverty, and they have become rich, but thanks to the fact that they managed, through intense mental work, to convert their energy into goods and products that are in great consumer demand
- If you are working hard and you are able to transform your energy in your chosen direction, sooner or later you will undoubtedly succeed, your efficiency, your effectiveness will increase

- In order to be successful in life, you must:
  - ➤ discover your latent energy;
  - ➤ start releasing it through labor;
  - ➤ direct energy in the right direction to the designated time to receive the expected result

SELF-EXAMINATION TEST

It should be noted only one answer is required for each question or statement. Accumulate points for each reply in accordance with the table at the end. Count the number of points.

1. **Are you convinced of the positive influence of school life for human development to reach certain positions in society?**

Yes.

No.

2. **In the achievement of your plans, do you feel well in the atmosphere of struggle and competition?**

Yes.

No.

3. **What are the characteristic features that are most important of the current political leaders:**

a. implementation of practical problems;

b. activities aimed at the protection of human dignity and the rights of citizens.

4. **Which of our activities should be regulated:**

a. the provisions of the religious materials;

b. ideas of beauty contests;

c. material considerations;

d. welfare.

5. For a friend, who would you choose:

a. A person enterprising, hard-working, endowed with a practical mind;

b. A person who thinks, dreamy and detached from reality;

c. A person with leadership and organizational abilities.

6. Is it enough to have the energy to overcome the difficulties encountered on the way?

Yes.
No.

7. Can we be glad that we live in such an active time?

Yes.
No.

8. Do you like to look into the fire?

Yes.
No.

9. Is it easy to carry on, when you have been refused, even if you know that your request cannot be met?

Yes.
No.

10. Are you a talkative?

Yes.
No

11. Do you live by this principle that every road leads to the goal?

Yes.

No.

12. Do you enjoy activities that require speed?

Yes.

No.

TEST RESULTS

№	YES	NO	A	B	C	D
1	5	-	-	-	-	-
2	5	-	-	-	-	-
3	-	-	5	-	-	-
4	-	-	-	-	-	5
5	-	-	-	5	-	-
6	5	-	-	-	-	-
7	5	-	-	-	-	-
8	5	-	-	-	-	-
9	5	-	-	-	-	-
10	5	-	-	-	-	-
11	5	-	-	-	-	-
12	5	-	-	-	-	-

From 0 to 40 points - Unfortunately, vigor is not your strongest quality. You quickly get tired, reluctant to take the responsibility, you keep your opinions to yourself, preferring to remain silent. You are full of indifference and cautious in dealing with others. Decision-making is giving you great difficulty. Your energy, as well as the ability to act depends on your imagination and not always well-founded fear. To be more effective, you should learn to direct your energy in a positive direction.

From 40 to 60 points - Not bad, you are an active and energetic man! You have different cheerful character, easy to get along with other people. However, you do not easily tolerate dependence on others (e.g., supervisors). You manage to surpass others in the energy and speed of decision-making, you are able to take responsibility for yourself. Your activity energy and dynamism allow you to be fully effective in your life and achieve impressive results!

PRACTICAL TASKS

1. Comment on what is a continuous cycle of transformation (conversion) energy. How does this help you to be more efficient?

2. What conclusions can be drawn from the life story of Henry Ford? What, in your opinion, has helped him to have a place in life and to succeed? Which of the lessons learned, do you intend to apply to your life?

CHAPTER 3:

HOW TO USE REPRODUC-TIVE ENERGY MORE EFFECTIVELY?

So, we are in the third chapter of the book called "DISCOVER YOUR SOURCE OF LATENT ENERGY." In the previous chapter we spoke to you about the continuous cycle of transformation (conversion) of energy. We remind ourselves that according to the law of conservation of energy, the total energy of an isolated system remains constant- it is said to be conserved over time. Energy can neither be created nor destroyed: rather, it is transformed from one form to another. In this chapter we will talk about how to make better use of our existing reproductive energy. I believe that what you have with you is very important to find out, to know what the true purpose of the reproductive energy is.

The most striking example of the energy inherent in us from the beginning, is the reproductive energy. According to the Dictionary of Russian synonyms "reproductive" means "self-replicating". Each of us from biology course in school, knows that people have a reproductive function. However, very few people reflect on this question philosophically. Did you know that today humanity has almost 7 billion populations? But let's see how it all began. At the beginning of our era on Earth was already 300 million.

By the end of the 1st millennium. n. e. - 400 million.

in 1500 – 500 million.

in 1820 – 1 billion.,

in 1900 – 1.6 billion.

in 1960 – 3 billion.

in 1993 – 5.65 billion,.

October 12, 1999 the world population was 6 billion.,

in 2003 – 6.3 billion.

in 2006 – 6.5 billion.

in 2010 – 6.8 billion,.

November 1, 2011 – 7.0 billion people. [12].

What began the gigantic scale of the growth of world population and amazing figures, was with only two representatives of humanity. That was the account given in the Bible, the oldest book of humanity - the Bible in Genesis 1, chapter 28, verse 29:

And God blessed them, and God said unto them, be fruitful, and multiply, and fill the earth and subdue it; and have dominion over the fish of the sea and over the birds of the air and over every living thing that moves on the earth.

And God said, Behold, I have given you every herb bearing seed, which is upon the whole earth, and every tree, in the which is the fruit of a tree yielding seed - to you [these things] shall be for food.

Thus, it only took two people for the entire human race to begin. At the same time God did not need to create all the billions of people he wanted to populate the earth. He acted very wisely to achieve the goal, He needed only to invest in the first two representatives of human, the energy to reproduce. The fact is that, in every human being lies this latent energy, and it means that this energy is enough for humans to reproduce their own kind. **That is why the Creator was satisfied to create only two people, but thanks to this inborn reproductive energy, they have multiplied and filled the whole earth.** Thus, the Lord God has begun a system that could function without His direct participation, performing the necessary task for Him.

Through the same reproductive energy, were all the land flora and fauna populated by God. He did not need to create a myriad of animals or plants, he simply put into each created being he desired, the reproductive energy, which, over time, has done its job. Latent energy is even in plants: from one seed grows a tree, from the tree, a whole forest. Also, due to the latent energy, a pair of animals was able to reproduce the whole herd, and a couple of birds - a whole flock. And now we have the opportunity to observe the fields and meadows, forests and steppes, a lot of flocks of birds and herds of cattle.

Thus, the power that enables us to automatically reproduce and recreate our own kind – is called the reproductive energy. But procreation - is only a small part of the action of the reproductive energy. **This source of energy is intended to be involved not only for procreation. Implementation of animal instinct - the instinct of reproduction (multiplication) - this is the lowest, most primitive level of human use of the reproductive form of energy.** After all, to live like an animal, do not need anything special - to create, to think, to meditate – it is just enough to act by instinct. If we only use the reproductive energy given as means of procreation, this is the lowest level of use.

WHAT MASLOW'S HIERARCHY SAYS AND WHAT IT DOESN'T?

People who think primitive implement only their own animal instincts - live at the lowest level of the reproductive energy, satisfy only their basic needs. When it comes to them, the modern society made reference to a hierarchical scale of needs -Abraham Maslow (1908-1970), one of the founders of human-istic psychology. Maslow proposed that healthy human beings have needs, and with detailed explanation and construction, that a person cannot experience a high level of demand, while in need of more primitive things. Abraham Maslow recognized that people have many different needs, but also believed that these needs can be divided **into five main categories:**

1. **Physiological Needs: hunger, thirst, sexual desire, and so on.**

2. **Safety Needs: comfort, stability of living conditions.**

3. **Social Needs: social communication, communication, affection, caring for others and giving attention to oneself, a joint operation.**

4. **Esteem Needs: self-esteem, respect of others, recognition, success and high scores, career growth.**

5. **Spiritual Needs: self-actualization, self-expression, identity, knowledge.**

"It is quite true that man lives by bread alone — when there is no bread. But what happens to man's desires when there is plenty of bread and when his belly is chronically filled? At once other (and "higher") needs emerge and these, rather than physiological hungers, dominate the organism. And when these in turn are satisfied, again new (and still "higher") needs emerge and so on. This is what we mean by saying that the basic human needs are organized into a hierarchy of relative prepotency "[13].

He called it hierarchical order of needs because they are arranged in the ascending order - from the lower (material) to higher (spiritual). To get to the highest requirements, which are - self-actualization, a person must meet the physiological needs, the need for security, love, respect, knowledge and aesthetic needs (harmony, beauty).

It is believed that the advantage of the concept of Maslow in his "spring motive" - the principle of hierarchy: the needs of each new level become important (vital) only after previous need have been satisfied. Physiological requirements are primary and perform dominant behavior as long as they are not satisfied at the least minimum level, they then begin to dominate demand on other levels - security, etc. Consequently, without satisfying their nutritional needs (as is known, they can... be different from porridge in the water, or, sandwiches with butter and red caviar), not having received the love of a partner or children, respect for others, self-realization is impossible. And here there will be the violation of priorities.

For a person created by God, the basic needs should be the realization of divine purpose in his life, to live in peace with God and inner harmony, the presence of health and a high level of internal energy. Such a person fulfills his physiological needs by being able to know how to deal effectively with self-actualization, realization of his mission. Having the opportunity to be engaged in business of his life is a priority for this person. In other words, he does not live to eat, he eats to live and to do something that is intended.

Of course, on an empty stomach there is not much to do, with no one to help, the dream cannot be realized. That is why Abraham Maslow wrote about the importance of meeting the physiological needs at least minimum level. The danger is that Maslow's concept can serve as a cover for selfish, lazy people who wait until their needs are fully met. A person who has no purpose does not know the calling, may justify himself by saying that he is not satisfied with the lower demand, and without meeting them, as we know, it is impossible to reach the highest spiritual search. **"Calling, says such a person - and he needs to earn money."** Everything is completely different for a person created in the image and likeness of God. And they do not relate to physiological need, when it comes to basic requirement of life. The word "man" implies a more inherent meaning, values that should be highlighted, displacing physiological need into the background. This person, a person who restrains his excessive desire, learning to be content with little. Otherwise, in what way is the man different from the animal, if in all his life's pursuit is directed towards how he will satisfy his physiological needs?

If a person does not have children, does this mean, according to Maslow's concept that he could not go to the next level, where he can develop his reputation, career, vocation? If a person is unable to eat well, surely he would not be able to think about dealing with people. A real man, not even having produced offspring, draws his strength and energy from the fact that he is alive and well, that his hands and legs are intact, he has a head on his shoulders, and he can earn a living. Because this person is healthy he is grateful in every circumstances.

Furthermore. Maslow argues that the satisfaction of higher needs is dictated by meeting the requirement for the lower need. For example, a person does what he likes, learning to build relationships, getting material benefit, having a good reputation, achieving success in his career, and this in order to improve his need for safety, or to increase his need for comfort. Now he can live in a penthouse, and instead of borscht, (French delicacy). So, people, reaching even higher degree of satisfaction of their needs, so no less, remained at the animal level.

A self-actualized man achieves success building relationships with people, he realizes a calling, on the basis of the moral principles, ideals values inherent within him. Perhaps all that is in his lunch - a plate of borscht, but he is satisfied with his life and successfully building relationships, realize his potential, to use his gifts and talents for the good of the people, without putting before him the question of remuneration as indispensable. Such a person lives from the inside out. Among self-actualized people the same Maslow attributed Albert Einstein,

Abraham Lincoln, Eleanor Roosevelt, Aldous Huxley, Thomas Jefferson, Jane Adams, William James, Albert Schweitzer and Baruch Spinoza, that is, those who have achieved success in life, living for a higher purpose and calling for fulfilling their mission. An important truth that you need to remember is this: if someone could do something once, then it can be done by the other person, many times. On the other hand, **if someone in the world in general could do anything, for example create, through the creative energy that lies initially in every human being, the same energy is in you, and it implies that you can do the same.** What do I mean by this? ACCEPT THAT EVERYTHING IN THIS WORLD IS CREATED AND WORKS ACCORDING TO THE LAWS, RULES AND PRINCIPLES. Even 1000 years ago, it was widely spread, the belief that not everyone is given the ability to read and write, know the alphabet, but now we all know that, that's not true. About 100 years ago only a few people, is thought that to have driven a car in the whole world. But today it's so funny to hear about it. About 20 years ago, many people were convinced that only experts can use a computer, but nowadays this myth successfully debunked. Thus, if someone is able to achieve something in this life, the success can be repeated by another person. Success or a place in life - this is not a mystical thing, not a matter of chance or providence: "Someone is given, and someone not, someone lucky, but if I'm lucky - is still unknown, because my whole life had no luck ... " The only question is whether you will be able to DISCOVER WITHIN YOU THE HIDDEN SOURCE OF ENERGY. It is the realization of that dream, that idea, the nature that we have from the Creator, that is most important thing or cause, for which our reproductive energy should be directed towards. This colossal immeasurable power - energy - is already in you. All you need to do - is to discover this for yourself and tap into its benefit, and create something extraordinary!

THE TRUE PURPOSE OF REPRODUCTIVE ENERGY

Reproductive energy is not only for the purpose of reproduction, but it can be applied in every aspect of life. This applies to all that we do, and most importantly, to why? Ask yourself if now, when there will not be, how to live, what do you do? To understand what I mean, think about what you know about your great-grandfather, about your great-grandparents at least four generations ago? What did they do? For what purpose did they live and what were they able to create? Does anyone remember their names for anything significant? Most likely, you do not remember and do not know the names of your ancestors. This is because they did not live, but just exist in this world; it is very important for us to live consciously, and build so as to leave a legacy that will live on for centuries.

I am afraid that many of our causes will not withstand the test of time, if we continue to do things the way we do them now. We must put ourselves in everything we do, what we do, so that when we die, our work system brings even more results and fruit than in our lifetime. OUR PROBLEM – IS TO CREATE SYSTEMS THAT WILL LAST FOR CENTURIES. To achieve this, we must consciously build systems with reproductive energy. It is in us, and we must act as God acts himself.

Do you know, dear reader, The Europe we now know today had always been like that? That European civilization as we know at the moment, the European values to which we are seeking today, in fact, were the product of reforms that took place in the fifteenth century. The most outstanding representatives of that era, whose names are known to us - were Luther, Calvin, Zwingli. But there were many unknown heroes who accelerated the arrival of the modern times in Europe, they include Wycliffe, Žižka, Jan Hus, and others.

As a result of their activities, the Reformation affected not only the church, but also social life and public way of the mainstream European countries. The Germans, who were reputed for being drunkards and optional people, acquired such pedantic quality and love for order. Without these qualities, the German nation will be hard to imagine. "German pedantry", "German order" - perhaps these words are familiar to each one of us, dear reader? Why is Switzerland famous for her precision to timing and the reliability of their banking system? - All this are as a result of the Protestant reformation. Though, it took almost 500 years for the transformation to be evidential, but the legacy left behind lived for centuries, even after the death of the reformers.

Rank	A country
1	Norway
2	Switzerland
3	Canada
4	Sweden
5	New Zealand
6	Denmark
7	Australia
8	Finland
9	Netherlands
10	Luxembourg
11	USA
12	Ireland
13	Iceland
14	Germany
15	Austria
16	United Kingdom

Indicators of living standards - the complex and multi-piece data, depending on many factors. But nonetheless, even in a simplified form in the countries situated rating follows [14]: Countries that are represented in this list – are the country dominated by Protestantism. The character trait clearly enshrined in them is the low level of corruption, the Protestant work ethic and respect for human rights. There you will see that sloppiness and carelessness, which were the rule rather than the exception in the CIS countries, united by a common socialist past. Even if you do not believe these reports, then surely you know the mindset of the majority of citizens of the country in which you live: in some states, they tend to get a better life, most of them flock to the pursuit of happiness in the countries is on this list. Few of them fear for the security and safety of life as in Swaziland and Burundi.

And the reason why these countries are like, "paradise islands" on this earth for someone, is not whether they are special countries where people were just lucky. No! in the history of these countries, there were people who thought about the basis of the values upon which they were built, through the administration of the State. These values and rules were taken from the Bible: Do not kill, do not steal, do not lie. That is why they were able to lay the foundations for a healthy society, which is now enjoyed by their children, and this model of society are the kind we so much desperately seek – we are the descendants of people who did not think deeply about how to build a society on a regular basis.

They used the latent energy contained in the Word of God, and because of this, were able to transform the society in which they lived. For example, before the radical changes that were brought by the reformers, it was strictly forbidden to read the Bible. So the first thing the reformers did was to make sure that access to the Word of God was provided to the largest possible number of people, in which lies the hidden energy of incredible power. Man - this is the image and likeness of God, that he has divine energy within himself, and that energy was enough to transform society.

God is the Creator, and each of us are privileged to be endued with this awesome ability that makes us also to be co-creators and with creative energies. Believing in this, the reformers used the creative energy to transform society. That is, the values of truth contained in the invisible, spiritual world, the Word of God, were released in the physical world by bringing the reality of heaven, at least in part, in their society. But the strength of this creative power was so great that it continued to have effect even after the death of the initiators of these changes.

Dear reader, you too can change the world! And such global changes that can spread literally all over the world can start with just one person, as was the case with Martin Luther. The impact of one person is hard to deny, no one can argue with the fact that through his life this world had taken different turn, it did not remain the same. Each of us can change the society in our generation, simply by detecting the source of stored energy within us. When the Freedom Fighters on the African continent discovered the hidden power within them, they fought for the independence of their countries and were able to change their world. Mother Teresa - a fragile woman could change the world, when she discovered and started to use the energy hidden in love.

Reformation that transformed Europe, established for centuries, the right values in the society that continues to live after their death. Now rarely will Europeans have to pay the price for the comfort they enjoy now, due to the efforts of their ancestors the reformers. In America, people also paid a price for a brighter future for their children, building a society based on Biblical values. America is currently one of the most desirable countries to which people emigrate from around the world. But it was not always so.

The new political system was formed in the struggle for independence from colonial Britain, the country was torn between the slave-owning South and the North, which was categorically against this unit of society. One of the prominent founding fathers of the United States, who played a key role at the base of the American States, in particular, in the conquest of independence and the establishment of the principles of a new political system, was Benjamin Franklin (1706-1790), he affixed his signature to all three important historical document that underlined that, the US as an independent state: the Declaration of independence, the US Constitution and the treaty of Versailles of 1783 (second treaty of Paris), which formally ended the war for the independence of the thirteen British colonies in North America from the UK.

Nothing in the natural course of things contributed to Benjamin Franklin's name being in the annals of history, for him to leave such an impressive mark in the hearts and minds of not only his contemporaries, but also distant descendants. He was the 15th of 17 children in the family that emigrated from England. As craftsmen, their income was derived through the production of soap and candles. Benjamin Franklin had to get himself, self-educated, as money from his father only lasted for two years of training him. At the age of 12 years Franklin began his career. How did he manage to escape beyond slavish existence, the purpose of which is the basic survival: to feed and clothe himself and his families?

In 1727, Benjamin Franklin established his own printing press. From 1729 to 1748 he published "Pennsylvania newspaper", and from 1732 till 1758 - Yearbook of "Poor Richard's Almanac." In 1728, He pioneered and was first president of The Academy and College of Philadelphia which opened in 1751 and later became the University of Pennsylvania. He organized and was the first secretary of the American Philosophical Society and was elected president in 1769. Franklin became a national hero in America when, as an agent for several colonies, he spearheaded an effort in London to have the Parliament of Great Britain repeal the unpopular Stamp Act. An accomplished diplomat, he was widely admired among the French as American minister to Paris and was a major figure in the development of positive Franco-American relations. His efforts to secure support for the American Revolution by shipments of crucial munitions proved vital for the American war effort.

He was promoted to deputy postmaster-general for the British colonies in 1753, having been Philadelphia postmaster for many years, and this enabled him to set up the first national communications network. After the Revolution he became the first US Postmaster General. He was active in community affairs, colonial and state politics, as well as national and international affairs. From 1785 to 1788, he served as governor of Pennsylvania. Although he initially owned and dealt in slaves, by the 1750s he argued against slavery from an economic perspec-

tive and became one of the most prominent aboli-tionists.

His colorful life and legacy of scientific and polit-ical achievement, and status as one of America's most influential Founding Fathers, have seen Franklin honored on coinage and the $100 bill; warships; the names of many towns; counties; educational insti-tutions; corporations; and, more than two centuries after his death, countless cultural references.

Why was he thinking about the structure of society, and cared much about human rights? He lived longer than many of his contemporaries, even than many of us in the 21st century where the living conditions are much better, and we cannot spend so much time dealing with domestic issues. After all, just think, in his time there was no electricity, no computers and other office equip-ment. What enabled him to live those high ideals? What enabled him to do so much that humanity still remem-bered his name with gratitude and admiration?

When Benjamin Franklin died in April 1790, at his funeral there were about 20 thousand men. Americans, and the world, are still remembering his work, even though he was never a President of the United States. At the World Peace Council Decision, Franklin's name was included in the list of the most prominent representa-tives of humanity. [15] What legacy do you want to leave behind after your life, dear reader? This will be expen-sive, your name? We, as Benjamin Franklin, are called to live more than the satisfaction of our natural needs. **The focus of our reproductive energy should be on creating and building what will outlive us even after we are gone.** So, I want to the end the third chapter of the book called "discover your source of latent energy." In this chapter, we addressed the issue of the reproductive energy: what is it and how to use it correctly. In the next chapter, dear reader, we will know, how to manifest creative energy in its fullness – this is, the second form of energy, by which the Creator has endowed us with. We will examine in detail the reason for the lack of ideas, and how to learn, no matter what, to generate new ideas.

THE GOLDEN NUGGETS

- Creator was satisfied to create only two people that, due to the inborn reproductive energy, they have multiplied and filled the whole earth

- Latent energy is even in plants: from the seed is a tree formed, and from a tree is a forest developed.

- Implementation of an animal instinct - the instinct of reproduction (multiplication) - is the lowest, most primitive level of use of humanity reproductive form of energy

- People who think primitive, implement only their own animal instincts - live at the lowest level of the reproductive energy, satisfy only their basic needs

- Reproductive energy acts not only in the reproduction of their own kind, but also in all our affairs

- It is necessary to put all of ourselves in all that we do and what we do, so that when we die, our work system brings even more results and fruit than in our lifetime

- Our task - is to create a movement or system that lives for centuries

- Our energy in the reproductive life should be focused on creating and building that will outlive us even after our death

SELF-EXAMINATION TEST

"Maslow's hierarchy"

This test will help you understand the hierarchy of your needs. At what level of awareness you are. How to fill: Answer the 20 question, indicating the degree closest to you - all this applies to your own opinions, visions and points of view. Answers evaluate letters that indicate:

C = absolutely true and accurate

M = more correctly and accurately

P = partially true and accurate

S = somewhat correctly and precisely

N = absolutely not true

1. Quiet operation - the most important thing for me	C	M	P	S	N
2. I prefer to work independently on my own	C	M	P	S	N
3. High salaries - the best evidence of human values in the company	C	M	P	S	N
4. Search for what makes me happy - the most important thing in life	C	M	P	S	N
5. For safety reasons - not the most important factor for me	C	M	P	S	N
6. My friends mean more to me than anything else	C	M	P	S	N
7. Most people think that they are better than they actually are	C	M	P	S	N
8. I want to have a job that would allow me to learn something new and develop my skills	C	M	P	S	N

9. Regular income is what I can count on as crucial for me	C	M	P	S	N
10. It is better to avoid very close relationships with colleagues	C	M	P	S	N
11. My self-esteem is more important to me than someone's opinion	C	M	P	S	N
12. The pursuit of a dream - it is a waste of time	C	M	P	S	N
13. Good work should include a good planned retirement	C	M	P	S	N
14. I Prefer job that involves communication with other people: clients and colleagues	C	M	P	S	N
15. I get angry when someone appropriates the work done by me	C	M	P	S	N
16. To go farther, to set my own limits - that's what motivates me	C	M	P	S	N
17. The most important aspect of the work in the company - good health insurance plan	C	M	P	S	N
18. It is important for me to be part of a cohesive group	C	M	P	S	N
19. My achievements give me the right to respect myself	C	M	P	S	N
20. I feel better when I do what I can, than when trying to perform something new	C	M	P	S	N

Count points

On the contrary, for every answer you put the letter that best meet your behavior. In the table below you'll find the number corresponding to the letter chosen for each of the 20 statements. For example, if, in response to the assertion of one, you have selected the letter "R" - this corresponds to the number "3" in the table "1" square.

1	2	3	4
C=5 M=4 P=3 S=2 N=1	C=1 M=2 P=3 S=4 N=5	C=5 M=4 P=3 S=2 N=1	C=5 M=4 P=3 S=2 N=1
5	**6**	**7**	**8**
C=1 M=2 P=3 S=4 N=5	C=5 M=4 P=3 S=2 N=1	C=5 M=4 P=3 S=2 N=1	C=5 M=4 P=3 S=2 N=1
9	**10**	**11**	**12**
C=5 M=4 P=3 S=2 N=1	C=1 M=2 P=3 S=4 N=5	C=5 M=4 P=3 S=2 N=1	C=1 M=2 P=3 S=4 N=5
13	**14**	**15**	**16**
C=5 M=4 P=3 S=2 N=1	C=5 M=4 P=3 S=2 N=1	C=5 M=4 P=3 S=2 N=1	C=5 M=4 P=3 S=2 N=1
17	**18**	**19**	**20**
C=5 M=4 P=3 S=2 N=1	C=5 M=4 P=3 S=2 N=1	C=5 M=4 P=3 S=2 N=1	C=1 M=2 P=3 S= N=4
SUMM: SS	**SB**	**SE**	**SA**

Each of the four columns may receive at least 5 and a maximum of 25 points. The mark in 20 balls and more evidence that the reasons outlined in this column are very important to you. The number of points from 15-19 indicate that these motives are less important to you. 10-14 points suggests that the reasons outlined in this column is not of particular importance to you. Number of points below 10 - the reasons presented in this column, it does not matter to you.

TEST RESULTS

Maslow's hierarchy (Interpretation)
Safety and Security (SS)

In the first column of the questionnaire assesses the needs for safety and reliability. These needs are long term in comparison with the basic necessities of life. Concerning the work, we usually talk about economic security and reliability of the comfortable conditions of life and sense of security. In the US, companies usually give to these needs, the money that is paid in return for work done by employees. In other countries, such as Japan, many companies offer employees housing, health clinics services (by the company), as well as provide a service to other specific requirements for safety and reliability. The American companies raised wages are often used to reward exceptional performance, and it may have a certain effect on the needs of security and reliability. But as workers living in different circumstances, payment may not always be the motive for these needs. When it seems that the payment may motivate the work execution (and it is not entirely uncommon) - this is because the money is also used to meet other needs and requirements, to motivate other remaining categories. The need for safety and reliability are particularly important for workers who are under threat of loss of work as a result of poor performance, or any other causes beyond their control.

Belonging to the society and demand (SB)

The second part of the questionnaire focused on the interaction between man and society, a sense of belonging and the need to be in demand. This means that effective interpersonal relations are necessary. The manager must create an environment where staff cooperation is rewarded. Only inexperienced boss can remember all the names and nicknames of their fundamentals subordinates, but usually he does not have time to establish a very close relationship with a large number of subordinates. To meet the needs of this kind, may be, the most efficient use of productive social motivation by working in groups or teams. This creates a situation in which, one carries out work in close cooperation with the other, a person satisfies his need to be in demand in society. This also has its advantages - no need to carry out socialization at work (useless conversations, and the like), which often has a bad effect on the quality of work. It is better to use a different approach to help reinforce the motivation associated with the need to be in demand by society. You can use the briefings and meetings (held once a week or more), as well as a formal system of delegation of the team. There are many ways to maintain social interaction in the team.

Self-esteem (SE)

Many people, perhaps even most, are motivated by the search for sense of the importance in themselves as individuals. This is the third category of the human motivation, what Abraham Maslow calls- the need for self-esteem. Obviously, management should praise employees for good work or for special achievements. It is also possible to organize the work so that people get a chance to feel that their efforts that brought results. This is one of the important sources of self-esteem. Also, the manager can arrange the work so that the worker will monitor their activities. This ensures that the results will be "owned" by the employee. Work should also be somewhat "integrated": a clear beginning and end, when they achieved results or when the actual product works, attest to its implementation. Many of the job, of course, are insignificant, and managers can bet that you cannot do every little task in a "great work." For partial solution to these problems can be used for teamwork. In this case, the overall achievement of the team will be perceived as an achievement of each of its members. Using a command that has a certain responsibility in the work, you can link the two motives - the demand for a society and a sense of self-esteem. There are many other kinds of recognition that can be used to meet the needs of self-esteem: the formal ceremony, like "Employee of the Month", a record of productivity on a bulletin board, praise at meetings, etc. - It all depends on the imagination of the head.

Self-actualization (SA)

The last part of the questionnaire focused on human motivation at the highest level (on Maslow) - The need for self-development, an attempt to become what people can be. Maslow calls this phenomenon "self-realization". Most people want to realize themselves to some extent, but to what degree? – it all depends on each individual. With self-actualization, the employee will be interested in growth and individual development. He will also need to be skilled at what he does. He may want a challenging job, an opportunity to complete further education, increased freedom from supervision, or autonomy to define his own processes for meeting organizational objectives. At this highest level, managers focus on promoting an environment where an employee can meet his own self-actualization needs. Managers should be mindful of such motivations, trying to constantly develop their subordinates. This can be done by planning staff development activities through formal training, instruction of complex tasks, the installation of new goals - everything that a manager can do for the development and growth of their subordinates.

Level	Security	In demand	Self - esteem	Self-realization of reliability
Very High	24	24	24	25
High	22	21	21	23
Average	18	18	18	20
Low	14	13	14	16
Very low	9	8	8	11

Safety / Reliability: very high = 24-25; high = 21-23; average = 16-20; Low = 13-15; very low = 5-12.

Demand for the company: very high = 23-25; high = 20-22; average = 15-19; Low = 12-14; very low = 5-11.

Self-satisfaction: very high = 23-25; high = 20-22; average = 16-19; Low = 13-15; very low = 5-12.

Self-actualization: very high = 25; high = 23-24; average = 18-22; very low = 5-14.

PRACTICAL TASKS

1. Which principle did God established in each of His creation? Why did not He just create a billion people, or flocks of birds and herds of animals? Why was God limited to two representatives to give rise to the entire human race?

2. Did you see that you are activating the reproductive energy, which, in addition to reproducing children, is designed to serve higher purposes: can "giving birth to" new ideas be creative? Do you agree with the fact that not only the great writers and artists can do it but you also, because in each of us lies God's nature? Write down how you can use your reproductive energy inherent in you to improve the world.

CHAPTER 4:

HOW TO DISCOVER YOUR CREATIVE ENERGY IN ALL ITS FULLNESS?

Imagination - is the beginning of creation. You imagine what you desire; you will what you imagine and at last you create what you will.

- George Bernard Shaw (1856-1950), Irish playwright, novelist and Nobel Prize winner

So, in the third chapter of the book titled "DISCOVER YOUR SOURCE OF LATENT ENERGY," we examined in details the kind of energy called reproductive energy. In this chapter we will examine in greater details, the creative energy. The questions that will be answered, will be as follows:

- What is the reason for the lack of ideas?

- How to learn to produce ideas?

Do you still remember that according to the law of conservation of energy, the total energy of an isolated system remains constant, it is said to be conserved over time? This means that the energy is never created nor destroyed: rather, it is only converted from one form to another, which means that it is always available. It is important to further understand everything about what will be discussed below.

In above we talked about the fact that we are designed to manifest the nature of God, inherent in us. But I want to tell you this, dear reader: we do this only when WE BUILD UP AS HE DOES - big and creatively produce and create more useful things than what have been known to us so far. That is, in addition to the reproductive energy, from birth, the man has been endowed with the wonderful powers: To

- Do
- Invent
- Dream
- Create

It says that each of us, **without exception, have a creative, or, in other words, the creative energy.** The above capacity is the potential we have, because we are His image and likeness in totality. Therefore, whatever the Lord is doing, that's what we are called to do as well. Creator Himself has creative energy: He always comes up with something: look, the kind of diversity in the world around us – everything He created is so unique, awesome and wonderful! You have this capacity in you, this inherent imagination! As far as it is revealed in us!

God has placed in every human creative ability, creative energy so that he can do, he can become a co-creator through - his life, new projects and initiatives. And this energy and ability is in everyone. But what is the reason why a person works and put this ability to use in a way that he become a living witness of someone who is a creative genius, and a friend who is just like him would agree that he is endowed with creative energy, and no one hear anything recorded in that friend's name. What is the reason? On what factor does it depend? What is the difference between these two people?

The difference is that his friend did not discover his force of latent energy – he did not work on them. What does it mean to "work on oneself"? In order to create, you need to acquire knowledge and skill to use your energy to turn word into substance. In order to create, you need to stop the flow of energy that is transmitted through you, and focus it on yourself, to acquire inspiration for wonderful ideas. Then the idea is painted as a picture in the mind, finding the real features, so you can paint the process of realization of this dream into achievable plans. The most recent and necessary step will be action, beginning at the implementation of the plan. Many people at this point don't have the patience nor the discipline to bring their plans to the fulfillment. But the one who can do it, becomes successful and famous. In George Bernard Shaw's words, he remarkably illustrates the process: «*Imagination - this is the beginning of creation. You imagine what you desire; you will what you imagine and at last you create what you will*» This is how all the great people have created their products, thanks to what became known all over the world.

Did you know that Benjamin Franklin was not only an outstanding leader, diplomat, but also a scientist, inventor, journalist and publisher? *His name is well known not only in connection with the founding of the American nation, as you read in the previous chapter. For example, he introduced what is now generally accepted designation of electrically charged states "+" and "-";*

- *Established the identity that the thunder cloud is produced by electricity of friction, and ascertained the proof of electrical nature of lightning;*
- *Established that the lightening rod, connected with the ground, can remove the electric charges from the thunder bolt even without touching them, and proposed in 1752 a draft diverter;*
- *Invented bifocals (1784);*
- *He received a patent for the design of rocking chairs;*
- *Invented an economical small-sized furnace for the house;*
- *He put forward the idea of an electric motor and has shown "the electric wheel" rotating under the influence of electrostatic forces;*
- *First used an electric spark for the explosion of gunpowder;*
- *Explained the principle of the Leyden jar, finding that the main role in it played by a dielectric separating the conductive plates;*
- *Improved glass harmonica;*
- *Developed its own time management system;*
- *Gathered extensive data on storm winds (north-east) and proposed theories to explain their origin;*
- *With his participation, the speed, width and*

depth of the Gulf Stream were measured, and eventually the mapping of the area in 1770.

Franklin wrote a number of works:
- *«Autobiography";*
- *«Discourse on freedom and necessity, pleasure and pain";*
- *«Experiments and Observations on Electricity";*
- *«The necessary advice to those who want to become rich";*
- *«The path to abundance";*
- *«simpleton Richard's Almanac";*
- *Letter-story "Whistle".*

In addition, we can say that Benjamin Franklin predicted the emergence of cryonics. Exactly 200 years after the presentation of his arguments about "traveling to Madeira cask" was cryopreserved first man [15].

You must consciously engage your mind and think how you can tap into the inherent gifts and abilities even more, and because by this, we glorify God, even better. To do this, you need to consciously deal with, work, learn to discover the artistic, creative energy, which is already in you. How do you manage this? It should be a source of creativity, creative energy - and at the level of the church, the city, the country, the world, the whole planet. Ideas - that's what we need, that what is vitally important!

One man came for janitor work in the company "Microsoft". The personnel department asked the man a few questions, and then conducted a small test, and finally announced:

- You have got the job. Leave your email address, they said, and let us know when you ready to go to work.

- But I have no computer, - said the man in confusion - not even an email address.

- In that case, we cannot employ you to work, because you virtually do not exist.

The upset, man went outside. In his pocket he had only 10 dollars. Asked himself how do I earn money? And then an idea came. He bought 10 kg of tomatoes from a farmer, and then sold the goods from house to house. In less than 2 hours, he managed to double the initial capital. After 6 hours of work in his pocket it was $ 160. And he realized that such income is quite possible to do without necessarily being employed in a company. After some time of working diligently, he bought a car, then a truck, then opened a shop, and five years later had already owned a chain of supermarkets. And then he decided to insure his life. After the initial talks, the insurance agent asked him to leave the email address so as to send the best offer to the merchant, the merchant replied just as he did few years ago, that he had no email address or even a computer.

- It's amazing, - said the insurance agent - you have such a big business - and there is no e-mail! Just imagine, what would you have become if you had a computer!

Kommersant said:

- I would have been a janitor for "Microsoft" company.

An idea - is what saved the man caught in a seemingly hopeless situation. Acting as standard, you'll have the standard result: there is e-mail – you get a job, there is no E-mail – you do not get. But maybe there is something that is beyond the scope of the proposed schemes and rules. And this is something, this new turn, will bring you much more profit and opportunities than if you stay in a peaceful and stable position of the status quo.

REASON FOR LACK OF IDEAS

Do you know why you often don't have ideas, there is no (or rather "sleeping", remains unclaimed) creative energy? **The only thing that kills this energy in us - is to be preoccupied with yourself, self-centered-ness. Egocentrism directed against the nature of God.** Nature of the Creator - is love, and giving love? He always thinks about how to create, to help, to make the case for good. While a self-centered person is only thinking about his problems. IF YOU THINK ONLY OF YOURSELF AND YOUR PROBLEMS, YOU HAVE NO TIME TO CREATE. YOU ARE CAGGED IN YOUR-SELF, YOU SEE NOTHING BUT YOURSELF. You are blinded by your countless problems and troubles, filled with self-pity, and thereby impairing your vision, your creative and reproductive energy – is inhibited. You stay by yourself, nothing is born in you! You become poor and the poor inside, so you see only problems, confusion and trouble.

The greatest gift you can give yourself - is to forget about yourself, think less about "yourself beloved,"

and think more about people, about new projects, the things that can bring light not only in your life, but to other people. GO BEYOND YOUR OWN PROBLEMS AND SORROWS, YOU STOP NOTICING ONLY YOURSELF AND BEGIN TO DISCOVER, POSSESS AND RELEASE YOUR CREATIVE ENERGY. And then, you will be exposed to the sea of new ideas!

George Washington Carver (c. 1864-1943), American botanist, mycologist, chemist, educator, teacher, his reputation is based on the research that made him to develop alternative crops to cotton, such as peanuts, sweet potatoes and soybeans. He invented over 300 ways for the use peanuts, except peanut oil. Due to his activities as a scientist-botanist, south of the US economy experienced a revival, and thousands of ordinary Americans were rescued from starvation [16].

Carver was likely born in January or June of 1864. His exact birth date is unknown because he was born a slave on the farm of Moses Carver in Diamond, Missouri, at a certain time when the American civil war was raging. When George was only a few weeks old, Confederate raiders invaded the farm, kidnapping George, his mother and sister. They were sold in Kentucky, and only George was found by an agent of Moses Carver and returned to Missouri. Carver and his wife, Susan, raised George and James and taught them to read.

When George was ten years old, he began to show great interest in nature, spending a lot of time in the meadows and in the forest, studying every blade of grass and every flower. But to become a scientist, it was necessary to get an education. When his parents sent him to school, the boy was happy, even though it was far from home. Since George was black, white children bypassed his side did not want to associate with him. Some of his classmates thought that "black" has no place in school. But that did not stop George in his eleven years to become the best school student.

After high school, George decided that he wanted to study botany at the University, but none of the universities wanted, at that time, have among their students, a Negro. The young man did not give up and in the end, he was able to enroll in one university, where he received his degree. George became the head of the department at the same university and became the first person with black skin who have received higher education, and then the first black to have taught in the high school. However, this did not last long: Carver colleagues did not want to work with him because of his skin color.

As a scientist, George Washington Carver did good for so many people: thanks to him, the former wasteland turned into blooming gardens, and what was considered weeds - in food. He invented methods of crop rotation to preserve the nutrients in soil and discovered hundreds of new species of crops that can be used in agriculture [16].

George Washington Carver belonged to the category of people who indulge in self-pity who might have been lamenting their fate. Instead, this amazingly gentle and humble man continued to do his job, fulfilling his calling, and living in accordance with his purpose. He deliberately refused selfish focus on himself and his own problems, he did not feel sorry or blame God for his predicament. And that was what helped him move beyond the limitations and unleash the creative energy, which he had from his very birth.

A person may be deficient of new ideas also because he is empty on the inside; he did not have enough reservoir of knowledge. If you cannot get the clear picture in your mind the way out of a situation - whether it is in a scientific dilemma, financial issues or options for improving your kitchen design - that is, you do not have new ideas - this means that you are in a creative dead end, and that you lack of knowledge. If you do not see new opportunities around you, or you lack of new ideas, it is a sign that you do not have the necessary knowledge base, you have a hunger for information, which is an urgent need to satisfy.

Signs of an information hunger lies in the fact that a person wakes up in the morning and

- do not know what to do
- do not see new opportunities
- he has no new ideas (but normally new ideas should be produced at a minimum within 10-20 days).

What seems to be missing in this situation? You need to start reading - read everything, but especially in the direction of your calling and purpose. In other words, you need to take the time to educate yourself. When you enter into this process, you will find that you have new ideas. "You cannot solve a problem on the same level at which it originated. You need to rise above this problem, rising to the next level, "- said Albert Einstein. This means that in order to solve the problems confronting you and the problems before your goals, which to you now seem elusive, it is necessary to rise to a qualitatively new level in your knowledge. Thus, self-education will help you to produce new ideas and to find the ways to their realization and implementation.

HOW TO LEARN TO PRODUCE IDEAS?

New ideas do not come from sitting on the ground. Talk to people, observe the world, select the cells of the office, ask questions and try!

- Steve Jobs (1955-2011), an American entrepreneur, recognized as a pioneer in the era of IT-technologies

All great achievements and discoveries in life – are the result of concentration - thoughts, energy and attention. Why do we have few people that have developed new, brilliant ideas? This is because they have no time: they have no time to focus, once focused, once focus... Imagine: The first time in my life to hear about the effect of a magnifying glass, it was brought to my home, I took a magnifying glass and paper, went out and tried to focus the sun ray through the magnifying glass on the paper, but I forgot I needed hard to keep the glass in one place. I drove it on all sides, and nothing happened. This is the reason why people fail to achieve success or result. They are unable to focus their mind on one thing, their thoughts wander and run awry. They wished for something, hoped for something, but are not structured, the organizational framework of their mind is missing. **The effect of the concentration and strength appear when we take one topic, one word or one subject and reflect on it for a long period of time, being fully absorbed in it.** And when this process reaches a certain depth, then, just as the athletes opened a "second wind", it gives rise to them an explosion - discovery of new ideas and thoughts. And a qualitative leap - the knowledge, skills, achievements, which, in turn, acquires the features of something magnificent or perfect.

Without the concentration of energy, without the ability to maintain a high level of concentration new ideas are not born. This concentration on any subject of conversation, discussion, thinking, leads to a break-through - a qualitative leap, a transition to a new level of knowledge, skills and achievements. The ability to concentrate and focus, the ability to step back from everything, lies in the nature of a genius, and it's an important feature through which new ideas are conceived or generated.

One of the misconceptions regarding the creative process is the fact that people believe that, before you begin a work you need an inspiration. But it is a lie that can destroy your life, your talents, your abilities and your potentials. If you wait, until you will be inspired, before you work, it is very rarely you get inspired and or maybe at long intervals. Instead of waiting, I advise you to automatically turn up your creative mechanism. If you need to write something - sit down and write! Take a pen or a computer (it all depends on your level of "advancement"), and get out all you can. Fulfilling the familiar motion, you easily dispatched the brain in the right direction. DO NOT WAIT FOR MUSE, YOU NEED TO DEVELOP THE SKILLS FOR CREATIVITY.

If a person is able to focus, then it is easy to be inspired by the muse. This means that at the moment of inspiration concentration included. That is, we can automatically launch the mechanism of creativity to work, in whatever we were doing. Pablo Picasso (1881-1973), Spanish painter, sculptor, graphic artist, scene-painter, ceramist and designer, said: "Inspiration exists, but it comes at the time." That is, to have the visitation of a Muse, you must, at a minimum, get started and to plunge into it! **Any creative process, such as writing books can be put on stream, converted into a skill.** Many people do not agree in their head the possibility of doing something without inspiration. However, but this is possible.

· American writer Stephen King wrote 10 pages every day without a lunch break, and regardless of day of the week. Even holidays are no exception to the rule for him. This good habit has made him the most prolific writer. To date, sold over 350 million copies of his books [17].

· Ernest Hemingway (1899-1961) had his own productivity schedule - every day, the writer pointed out how many words are written (the figure varied from 450 to 1250). To do this he had to wake up early in the morning, in time to fulfill this quota before the sweltering heat and create in peace and quiet moment. It was said that Hemingway regarded his art

> more as a craft - the same share of poetry
> and pragmatism. [18]

Stephen King and Ernest Hemingway were not expecting any muse or inspiration. Even if the muse visited them, it is most likely due to their hard work and perseverance, thanks to the fact that they regularly sat in front of the desk and were given a certain portion of the written material. After that, you begin to understand the wisdom that is contained in the answer of Mark Twain (1835-1910), another American writer, in the following stories.

A young writer who was losing confidence in his literary talent. Once asked Mark Twain;

- Have you ever had a similar experience like mine? - asked the writer.

- Yes, - said Twain. – when I was fifteen years old, I wanted to write a book and I found out that I don't have the talent.

- And what did you do? you gave up writing? Asked the writer

- Do think I did? If I did then, by now I won't be a famous writer. Said Mark Twain

To become famous and well-known writer, you need not so much of talent as discipline, perseverance and high efficiency. For new ideas to come your way as often as possible, you just need to develop the skills to work on it regularly and consistently. No other way! It is one thing - to wait for the muse, and another thing - to turn it into a principle. Thanks to the tenacity and persistence, you can develop the specific skills that allow it to "generate" always into something new, without waiting for the muse. And then you do not have to wait for inspiration. Think: "As long as there is no inspiration, either before that, I cannot guess", - it is misleading. It should be self-induced, a burst for creativity, because it was originally present in us! This means that you do not have to wait, until the idea will fall on you from the sky – and then will overshadow you with its presence.

You need to motivate yourself to do something, just to put pressure of yourself and bring yourself to move, in spite of feelings and emotions, "squeeze" the energy, squeeze the juice of creativity out of you.

Remember the childhood time: no bike will start ridding itself, until you start pedaling. Only when there is a force pressing on the pedal, that energy is released to move the wheels. The same applies to a juicer: the juice is released only when the orange is under pressure. The same thing with energy: it is released when we push ourselves to move, not to sit and wait for the muse and inspiration. If you just sit and wait, we risk nothing to wait for.

You don't have to be great at something to start, but you have to start to be great at something "

**- Zig Ziglar (1926-2012)
made this statement**

The popular author, lecturer and consultant who has been awarded three honorary awards of the US Congress for the efforts made by him in the development of America's free enterprise, perfectly illustrated all of the above. YOU WILL NEVER ACHIEVE GREATNESS AND WILL NOT SUCCEED IN LIFE IF YOU DO NOT START TO RELEASE YOUR LATENT POWER, THAT

IS ALREADY HIDDEN IN YOU. And in order to start doing something in the direction of success and prosperity, for something to take place in your life, you may not necessarily start from a good position – it may not necessarily represent something extraordinary. **You can start from the place you are at today.**

In his book "D. Templeton 90 minutes. World laws of lif" John Templeton brings amazing story of a man who began his path to success and prosperity, just being on the street.

After serving for more that eighteen years in the U.S. Army, Sam was dishonorably discharged for drunkenness and fighting. It was difficult to convey by words, the depression and confusion, the man experienced to live on "citizen", he was not accustomed to, and can hardly imagine of what use he could find himself out of military service. The small amount of money he was able to accumulate during his service in the army, quickly ran out, and Sam began to live on the streets. Sam went to Vietnam war, but on the street, life was a different ball game, the ordeal there was inconceivable. "There, in a war, you know exactly who your enemy is, but on the street it is difficult to predict who will dump you on earth to steal your latest shoes."

One day, while waiting for lunch to be served at the church soup kitchen, Sam answered a call for volunteers to help move some furniture and roll up the rug that needed replacement. It was the first time he had done anything for anyone. It really felt good for him. As he was leaving the building after lunch, Sam noticed a heavy growth of moss on the roof that threatened to damage the shingles. He volunteered to remove it. "You are welcome to help, but you know we won't pay you", the supervisor said. Sam went ahead with the work anyway, and again an expected good feeling. Sam developed the habit of offering his services whenever he heard of a job he thought he could do.

When welfare centers needed a volunteer as an operator on the PC, they remembered about Sam. Once upon a time, even in the army, Sam learned to work on a typewriter, and now the ability is to be useful to him. The man responded enthusiastically to the invitation. Very quickly after Sam began his work in the office, he was able to leave the street and live in a free room in the house of one of his new colleagues. Then, without asking for it, the center manager offered him a small salary and increased his responsibility in the office. Another co-worker offered Sam a good used automobile for a reasonable price, with payment he could easily afford., Sam was assigned the management of the community food closet in the warehouse at the same charity to which he first volunteered... Now he can afford to have his own apartment and has plans to marry. Unveiling a new life, Sam believed that the positive changes in his life started when the people at the center began to believe in him. [19]

It is true that for others it was a step of confidence, but the first step had to be taken by Sam. By offering his services, Sam went into creative and productive flow of life. Having started to act, bringing in himself the movement, he led the countdown to a new season of his life. It turned out that there is a lot of variants that one can do in life, a myriad of ways and exits from those hopeless deadlock and the situations in which we find ourselves at times. With just one step in the right direction you start regaining your sapped energy back - to do what is in your power, that you now can do, you begin to open an incredible ocean of life energy, which is full of new ideas for you.

By developing the skills to urge yourself to move, to shift yourself from the "dead spots", you can continuously build and "produce" something new.

There is no need to wait for something to happen, all you need is already available in you, God is in you, his genes, his nature is already in you! That is why we are constantly developing new designs and making progress. There is no boring moment around us, so that in our life there is no stagnation, there is a constant movement. It all depends on how much you know and understand, HOW TO DISVOVER TO YOUR STORED ENERGY SOURCE. If you are constantly engaged in the study of any matter, to work on a specific problem, then eventually, the flow of new ideas in your chosen direction becomes a habit, a second nature. But it all begins with the fact that a person **is constantly in search of the new ideas.** Steve Jobs is not wrong to say that "new ideas do not come from sitting on the ground." It comes, in fact, to generate new ideas – is no big deal. In the process as you engage with various people, observing the environment, asking questions and trying to learn something new. **Most importantly - do not stay in one place, in a static state, but put yourself in the movement - the**

movement of thought, will and action. Get a great, successful, and influential - so easy!

So, in this chapter of the book entitled "DISCOVER YOUR SOURCE OF LATENT ENERGY," we examined in details this type of energy as a creative, the creative energy, thanks to the fact that each one of us can be the creator of new ideas, new projects, new social and political movements that could change the face of the earth in this generation. In the next chapter we will look at the phenomenon of back-up power. It will be very exciting, you will be encouraged and challenged. We will look into so many examples of people with unique abilities. The following, fifth chapter of this book, we will discover what steals our energy, and try to discover how to open a backup energy hidden on the inside of us.

THE GOLDEN NUGGETS

- Each of us, without exception, has a creative, or, in other words, the creative energy
- The only thing that kills this energy in us - is to be consumed with yourself, self-centeredness
- If you think only about yourself and your problems, then you have no time to create and develop yourself
- The greatest gift you can give yourself - is to forget about yourself, think less about "myself beloved," and to think more about other people, about new projects that could bring light not only in your life, but others.
- Just by going beyond our problems and sorrows, just by stopping to focus on ourselves, we begin to discover and release our creative energy
- In order not to wait for the muse, it is necessary to develop the creative skills
- Any creative process, such as writing books can be put on stream, converted into skill
- If someone was able to achieve something in this life, the success can be repeated by another person.

SELF-EXAMINATION TEST

It should be noted only one answer is required for each question or statement. Next to each answer marked point. Stacked score will determine the outcome of your training.

1. **Do you consider that the world around you can be improved?**

a. Yes - **2 points**

b. Yes, but only in some ways - **1 point**

c. No, it is already good enough - **0 points**

2. **You are free to participate in the significant environmental changes in your environment?**

a. Yes, in most cases - **2 points**

b. Yes, in some cases - **1 point**

c. No - **0 points**

3. **Is it true that some of your ideas would bring substantial progress in the field of your activities?**

a. Yes - **2 points**

b. To some degree - **1 point**

c. Yes, under favorable circumstances - **0 points**

4. **Do you think that you will continue to play such an important role that can fundamentally change something?**

a. Yes, for sure - **2 points**

b. Possibly - **1 point**

c.   Unlikely - **0 points**

5. When you decide to take some action, are you sure to exercise your initiatives?

a.   Yes - **2 points**

b.   Often I doubt - **1 point**

c.   No - **0 points**

6. Do you have a desire to get to work, which is absolutely unknown to you?

a.   Yes, you are attracted to the unknown - **2 points**

b.   It all depends on the nature of the case - **1 point**

c.   Unknown, you are not interested - **0 points**

7. In having to deal with an unfamiliar task. Do you have a desire to achieve perfection in it?

a.   Yes - **2 points**

b.   Yes, if you like it - **1 point**

c.   Satisfied with what achieved - **0 points**

8. If the case is that you do not know you like it, do you want to know everything about it?

a.   Yes - **2 points**

b. No, you just want to satisfy your curiosity - **1 point**

c.   No, you just want to learn the most basic - **0 points**

9. When you fail, then:

a.   You continue to do your job - **2 points**

b. Sometime persist illogically - **1 point**

c. Give up on the venture, because you understood that it is not realistic - **0 points**

10. In your opinion, the profession should be chosen on the basis of:

a. Its features, the future prospects for yourself - **2 points**

b. The advantages it provides - **1 point**

c. Stability of the profession, it needs - **0 points**

11. When traveling, can you easily navigate the route, which you have already passed?

a. Yes - **2 points**

b. Yes, but only where the terrain you are familiar with - **1 rating**

c. Not afraid to go astray - **0 points**

12. Immediately after a conversation, can you remember all that was said?

a. Yes, without difficulty - **2 points**

b. Memorize only what you are interested in - **1 point**

c. Often cannot remember - **0 points**

13. When you hear the word in a foreign language, can you repeat it without error?

a. Yes, without difficulty - **2 points**

b. Yes, but not quite right - **1 point**

c. Yes, if the word is easy to remember - **0 points**

14. In your spare time you prefer:

a. To be alone, to think - **2 points**

b. You do not care - **1 point**

c. Be in the company - **0 points**

15. Do you do anything. You decide to stop this occupation, when:

a. case is closed and you feel perfectly satisfied - **2 points**

b. You have not managed to do everything - **1 point**

c. You are more or less satisfied - **0 points**

16. When you are alone, then:

a. I try to find a particular lesson - **2 points**

b. I love to dream about things that relate to my work - **1 point**

c. I love to dream about some abstract things - **0 points**

17. When some idea grabs you, then you will think about it:

a. No matter where and with whom you are - **2 points**

b. Only where it is not too noisy - **1 point**

c. You can only do this alone - **0 points**

18. When you are defending an idea:

a. You keep to your own opinion, no matter what arguments you've heard - 2 points

b. You can abandon it if hear the compelling argu-
    ments of opponents - 1 point

c. Change your mind, if the resistance is too strong
    - **0 points**

TEST RESULTS

From 0 - 17 points - sorry, your creativity at the moment is small. Perhaps you simply underestimate yourself and your ability. Lack of faith in your own strength can lead you to believe that you are not able to work.

From 18 - 35 points - You have a very normal creativity. You have the qualities that allow you to do, but you have, allowed problems to impede the creative process. In any case, your potential will allow you to express yourself, if you are willing, of course, wish.

From 36 points – You are endowed with consider-able creativity that gives you a wide choice of creative possibilities. If you actually will be able to apply your skills, then you have access to the most diverse forms of creativity.

PRACTICAL TASKS

1. What is creative energy? Can you create? What was the last year that you have created something that lifted you to a higher standard of living? Record 10 factors that can hinder you in the development of your creative energy. Write 3 ways out of each of the factors that may hinder you in the development of your creative energy.

2. What did you learn from the story of George Washington Carver? What are the lessons you are ready to learn from his life and career path?

CHAPTER 5:

HOW TO UNLEASH YOUR RESERVED ENERGY?

Greetings to you, dear reader, in the pages of the next chapter of the book entitled "DISCOVER THE SOURCE OF LATENT ENERGY"! We will continue our exciting journey into the world of energy, and to remind you that the fundamental principle of our research is the law of conservation of energy, whereby energy is never and will never disappears and reappears, the total energy of an isolated system remains constant- it is said to be conserved over time. Energy can neither be created nor destroyed: rather, it is transformed from one form to another. I recall that in the previous chapter, we have the answer to the question of how manifest our creative energy. We also learned the reason for the lack of ideas and learning how to generate new ideas? In this chapter, we will focus on backup power.

Perhaps, dear reader, you could at least want to see the movie-drama "Rain Man" (1988), directed by Barry Levinson, which tells the story of suffering syndrome savant Raymond and his cynical brother Charles Babbitt. This picture has earned four "Oscar", "Golden Globe" and the "Golden Bear" at Berlin Film Festival. What is interesting in this film?.

The film tells the story of an abrasive and selfish young wheeler-dealer, Charlie Babbit (Tom Cruise), who discovered that his estranged father had died and bequeathed all of his multimillion-dollar estate to his other son, Raymond (Dustin Hoffman), an autistic savant, of whose existence Charlie was unaware. Charlie is left only his father's car and his collection of roses. Charlie then kidnaps Raymond and decides to take on a lust for life trip to the west coast as a threat to get the 3 million dollar inheritance.

It turns out that Raymond has a phenomenal memory and can solve complex arithmetic calculations with his mind. But at the same time on the mental development of a child Raymond recalls. He lives in his inner world, strictly following its own timetable. Charlie was to take the trip by flight to Los Angeles but Raymond refused, it turns out that Raymond is afraid to fly on airplanes, because he remembered by heart the number of victims of air crashes in recent years. As a result, Charlie has no choice but to make a road trip together with his brother and cross the whole of America, to get from Ohio to Los Angeles.

Travelling together as brothers was good for them: they have not previously known each other, they came together. First, specific habits and behavior Raymond was strongly irritated by intolerant and selfish Charlie, but even then he used unusual abilities of his brother-savant, so he manages to extricate himself from a difficult financial situation. At the same time, being close to his brother, Raymond starts to better navigate the world. By the end of the journey they developed a genuine friendship and affection.

During this time, Charlie learned that his father placed Raymond in hospital many years ago, after he accidentally poured boiling water a little Charlie. This causes him to reconsider his attitude to the deceased father, forgetting all the old resentments. Communication with Raymond and Charlie suddenly helps to restore the relationship with his girlfriend Suzanne. In the end, after talking to psychiatrists, Charlie agrees to return Raymond's clinic, where that would be safer and more secure, and he decides to visit his brother.

The film's title was not chosen by chance. According to the creators of this game of words: words of Raymond and Rain Man (English - Rain Man) are similar in pronunciation - also illustrated the relationship between the brothers. Charlie remembered that when he was a kid and what happened was terrible, he was visited by Rain Man, and sang songs to him, comforting him, he remembered that Raymond was actually a caring and loving brother and was able to recall the connection that they shared when they were young. Only now, after meeting his unusual brother and getting to know him, Charlie realized that it was Raymond who, calling slurred his name, turned in his memoirs in a magical Rain Man.

WHERE DOES THE RESERVE ENERGY OF AUTISTIC SAVANTS COME FROM?

Latent energy is clearly expressed in such phenomena as a syndrome or autistic savant. These people cannot do the usual stuff, but in something else they are developed better than anyone: perhaps they cannot by themselves go to the store or on their own take a bath, but they find it easy to do something that in our view can only be done by geniuses, what normal people cannot do at all. Although these people are inherently handicapped, BUT THEIR EXAMPLE BECOMES MORE VIVID AND EVIDENT AS DISCLOSED IN A SOURCE OF HIDDEN, BACK-UP ENERGY.

What is the savant syndrome or savantism? savant syndrome (French savant -. scientist) - a medical diagnosis that describes a person in a rare condition in which, having developmental disabilities, he has a so-called "island of genius" - that is, outstanding abilities in one or more areas of knowledge or creativity. The degree of possession of social skills in the majority of savants is reduced, so that they cannot lead a full life in society as autistic. Autism (Greek autos -. Itself,) is defined in medicine as a mental disorder characterized by immersion in the world of personal experiences, with the weakening or loss of contact with reality. In autism there is loss of interest in reality, there is no desire to communicate with others, and a paucity of emotional manifestations [20].

· The prototype of the hero Raymond Bebbita in the film "Rain Man", which we discussed earlier in this chapter, became famous Savant Kim Peek, who friends and family called **"Kim-puter."** This nickname he got by chance, because he can remember 98% of all the information that came within the scope of the field of his vision! For example, to read one page of text, Kim goes from three to eight seconds: from his left eye, he is able to read the page on the left and right - the one on the right. In fact, to read a book by Tom Clancy's "The Hunt for Red October" Kim Pico took only 1 hour 25 minutes. But that's not all: four months later, he could correctly name the Russian radio operator, as well as the page that corresponded to his description, and to quote a few paragraphs of text. [20]

Kim had a unique brain: he is able to, without hesitation call the reign of any monarch, quoted by heart the complete works of Shakespeare, having a photo-graphic memory, memorized the map of the whole US states. At 53 years, he knew by heart more than 7000 books, and a special delicacy feeds to directories and statistical tables. In addition, Kim can produce in his mind of the most complex mathematical operations: in the three years the strange genius was able to instantly retrieve the cube root and multiply three-digit numbers with decimal fractions [21].

· **Alonzo Clemons** – An American sculptor, is able to create very accurate animal sculp-tures out of clay. Clemons can create a sculpture of almost any animal, even if he has seen only a glimpse of it. He is also able to create a realistic and anatomically accurate three-dimensional rendering of an animal after looking at a two-dimensional image for a mere moment.

· **Steven Viltshir** - English architect, who participated in the experiment of the Air Force. Flying over London by helicopter, accompanied by two reporters a few minutes and returned to the studio, Stephen was able to draw an accurate map of the area of four square miles, with detailed accuracy painted about 200 buildings. Since childhood as an autistic patient, he was sick and up to nine years could not speak.·

· **Sarah Miller** - American programmer, president of «Nova Systems, which has the ability to find a" bug ", or an error in the program or system, only glancing at the code [20].

· Englishman **Christopher Taylor** perfectly learned 30 languages, just by reading foreign newspapers at the local pub.

· 12-year-old American **Matt Savage** – Autistic savant musician. Matt was a precocious infant who walked early and learned to read by age 18 months. He was diagnosed with pervasive developmental disorder, a form of autism, at age three. Matt did not like any noises or music during his early childhood. At age six, Matt taught himself to read piano music. He studied classical piano for less than a year before discovering jazz, which became his main focus. He began studying at the New England Conservatory of Music in Boston, Massachusetts in the fall of 1999. He continued his classical studies as well. He and his younger sister, Rebecca, were both home schooled. Among Matt's talents are Hyperlexia and perfect pitch. Coupled with his extremely high intelligence, these abilities have allowed him to achieve other distinctions as well, such as winning a state-wide geography bee. Despite his young age and hid autism, and even without formal education in musical composition, Matt is an accomplished musician and composer. He has released several albums, both as a solo and as part of Matt Savage Trio.

· It is known that in 1940 the elections to the US Congress working American "human calculator" **William Dayzart.** Speaking to radio listeners on the air, he immediately processed with his mind the result of the coming regional election and, giving a summary of the relationship between the political forces. To entertain the audience, Dayzart arithmetic prowess is demonstrated by counting the number of seconds from the time of birth, the year each candidate had lived. [21]

All these savants share one thing: they suffer from autism. For example, **Kim Peek** was unable to perform simple everyday actions that would ensure the replenishment of his personal needs, it was hard for him to remember a sequence of simple actions. Only after the film, the prototype of the hero which he was, Kim stopped to lead a secluded life, learned to communicate with people and to relate with other people, and later became a lecturer on psychology and medicine. **Stephen Viltshiru** a child diagnosed with autism, up to nine years, he did not speak. **Sarah Miller** in all business meeting needs the personal psychologist, who takes all the above with the universal language understandable only to her, special, bizarre binary language. She also autistic [20].

Very rare savant syndrome associated with outstanding ability to develop after a person has a serious injury or illness. Jason Padgett became a mathematics genius after brain injury as a result of the attack on him. *Two men attacked him, when Jason came out of a karaoke bar, the result was that he suffered from severe concussion and post-traumatic stress disorder. Before this incident, the young man was an ordinary furniture salesman, who had little interest in academics. After the injury, he developed the ability to visually represent mathematical objects and physics concept intuitively.*

The resulting injury unlocked part of his brain, that makes everything in his world appear to have a mathematical structure. Padgett says he sees all shapes and angles everywhere in real life: in the geometry of the rainbow, and in the fractals in the water spiraling down the drain. After the injury Padgett with his new vision, came an astounding mathematical drawing ability.

In addition, started sketching circles, composed of superimposed triangles, which helped him under- stand the principle of Pi - the ratio of circumference to its diameter. This young man sees all forms as the final designs of the smaller units, which in physics is called the Planck length, which is considered the shortest length measured, and precisely because he does not like the concept of "infinity". One day, a physicist spotted him making these drawings in a mall, and urged him to pursue mathematical training. Padgett went to university and became a theoretician in the field of numbers [22].

Thus, people with savant syndrome are able to:

- repeat several pages of text, having heard them only once;
- accurately determine the result of multiplying multi-digit numbers;
- say what day of the week it will be in 1 January 300;
- sing all the arias heard coming out of the opera;
- draw a map of the city after flying over it.

Imagine within each of us the amount of back-up energy we possess! Those abilities possessed by the savants, is not as a result of the fact that these sets of people are extraordinarily special or that they are specially endowed by this gift. Rather, it means that we don't release and do not use all the energy residing in us. In fact, we are almost not used to the fact that we have this deposit of energy, and that we have not incorporated this energy from the beginning.

We all have incredible reservoir of the latent energy. Those abilities that we manifest now, are only the tip of the iceberg. We all have hidden reserves, but it is believed that the average person uses between 3 and 5% of their intellectual energy, and not more than 15% of their physical energy. And what do we do with the rest, why don't we use the energy? It remains in reserve, while we complain that we are poor, powerless and incapable. And in fact, we are not poor and not incapable, the truth is that we have not taken advantage of, and tap into the wealth of the energy reservoir the is resident within us. There is an immeasurable reserve of energy in us, that if we tap into this resource of backup energy, we will be an amazement and the envy of our generation.

WHAT STEALS OUR ENERGY?

When we looked into the Internet, we do not read their horoscope and did not go on dating sites. We are interested in the search - the information that really affects people's lives

- Sergey Brin (1973), an American entrepreneur and scientist in the field of computer technology, information technology and the economy, the billionaire developer and co-founder (along with Larry Page), the Google search engine.

We cannot bypass our earthly life, it becomes sad, and abuse to our destiny if we cannot do anything significant of the earth. These autistic people exhibited outstanding abilities because their attention is not focused on mundane things, they don't worry about what to eat, what to drink and what you to wear. The routine care, which has dominated almost all our day to day activities and our eclipsed our thoughts, do not disturb the savants. They have no worries; hence they were able to develop these outstanding abilities. And our attention constantly wanders about, our focus shifts from the right issues and questions around us, we are constantly distracted by extraneous and unimportant things, so that the impact of our lives is close to zero. ADO, CARE, CONCERNS STEAL ALL OUR ENERGY.

While, our energy is wasted as a result of having too many issues to deal with, some irrelevant and some insignificant to our lives, the savants, energy is concentrated in one direction with a definite focus on a clear goal. This principle is applicable when a person loses sight or hearing, other senses are sharpened - such as touch. If a person is deprived of the opportunity to see, he remembers a lot more than the people around him. Why? Because by overlapping the channel of information from the outside world immediately mobilizes the other as if to compensate for the loss.

For example, deafness can go even for the benefit of man, because he is, in this case, is not distracted, his attention is not divided on extraneous and distracting noises and sounds.

For example, the great inventor, Thomas Edison, almost lost his hearing at the age of 14. Most likely, the reason was the infectious diseases. For someone else it would be a lifetime tragedy. Just imagine the kind of problems faced by people completely devoid of hearing! But it did not give a reason for Edison, to remain in the darkness of self-pity. Edison himself, later said that deafness served him good, instead: for most of the day he could work without the distraction of background noise, and when it comes to sleeping time he slept like the dead. [23]

From the above we can deduce an important lesson for our lives. Which is; **when we consciously and deliberately concentrate our energy on something, we can achieve all that we want, and we can achieve success in any field of activity, we desire!** There hidden energy in every one of us, and this invisible treasure can only be discovered through:

- concentration
- targeted self-development and improvement.

IF WE ARE LESS DISTRACTED AND WE DEVELOP MORE QUALITY OR VIRTUE, AND IT IS POSSIBLE TO ACHIEVE ALL OF WHAT WE COULD HAVE IMAGINED!

The ability for a high degree of concentration is also called the superior quality of great men. When our attention is focused, the energy of our activities or thoughts are not dissipated. Through concentration we can do great things! Concentration - this is the best quality that you can have in your life, this is what allows for the disclosure of your reserve capacity and energy.

Please once again paying attention to the words of Sergey Brin, which I took as an epigraph to the section of the chapter you are currently reading: *"When we looked into the Internet, we do not read horoscopes and did not go on dating sites. We are interested in the search - the information that really affects people's lives."* Sergey and his colleagues have a high degree of concentration in their approach to work. By accessing the Internet, they are not lost in his fathomless expanses for hours aimlessly surfing on the Web. They investigated and concentrated on the most important thing that related to the subject of their interest.

CONCENTRATION – THE KEY TO DISCOVERING AND RELEASING LATENT ENERGY

Isaac Newton (1642-1727), English physicist, mathematician, astronomer, and mechanics, one of the founders of classical physics made the following statement: **"Genius is patience – with thoughts concentrated in a certain direction."** This suggests that successful people are able to focus their attention on their goal for a long time – in all that we do in life; focus is the key to achieving the objective. Great achievers stay concentrated as long as the purpose - the desired result is achieved. Then focus is the key through which the great scientists could make scientific discoveries, thus ensuring scientific and technological progress and the advancement of human development. It is by concentration that incredibly new ideas and projects are born. **When we concentrate our focus on some fact, we release energy.** CONCENTRATION - THIS IS WHAT ENHANCES THE RESULT.

Kurt Vonnegut (1922-2007), American writer and satirist, one of the most important American writers of the XX century, claimed that "the secret of the success of any human activity is the total concentration." This ability accelerates our high performance in all our endeavors and aspirations. Surely, dear reader, you have heard of such great people like Sir Isaac Newton, Mikhail Lomonosov, Mendeleyev, Thomas Edison, Albert Einstein and many others. Each of them managed to reach the top in their field. And they all shared a common denominator to their success, which provided the breakthrough in the study, eventually allowed them to become pioneers and trailblazers, a qualitative leap in the development of mankind. That common denominator is, the ability to stay focused on one thought or object for a long period of time.

THE MORE A PERSON CAN CONCENTRATE, THE BETTER THE RESULT, THAT CAN BE ACHIEVED. **The degree to which you can concentrate and stay focused - that is, to keep your thoughts in one direction, and will determine the degree of your genius.** The longer you can "dig" and go into the subject of the study, the more genius you will be able to discover. Thus, the genius - the ability to hold your attention at one point, and, relatively speaking, to continue in this "action". Because only in this case you can see and discover what others cannot see, and achieve the impossible.

Thomas Alva Edison - the world-renowned American inventor and businessman, who perfected the telegraph, telephone, cinema equipment, built the first electric locomotives, marked the beginning of electronics, invented the phonograph, and one of the first commercially successful electric incandescent lamp options. When he was searching for a suit-

127

able material for incandescent light bulb, he went through about 6000 samples of the materials until his team discovered that a carbonized bamboo filament could burn for more than 1,200hrs. Checking the lamp characteristics of the coal chain, he spent in the laboratory for about 45 hours without rest. Up until very old age, he worked for 16-19 hours a day.

Nikola Tesla (1856-1943), the inventor in the field of electrical engineering and radio engineering, engineer, physicist, spoke well of his rival: "If Edison had to find a needle in a haystack, he would not waste time trying to determine its most probable location. On the contrary, with immediate feverish diligence, he will begin to examine straw by straw until he has found the desired result. " It was Thomas Edison who was the author of many important inventions: in his lifetime the US Patent Office has issued about 1093 patents in his name – this was an extraordinary feat for one person to receive so much patent (!).

Do you think that the public showing of Edison occurred randomly, making him one of the greatest men of our time? I do not think so. Edison was an outstanding example of a purposeful, persistent and focused person and scientist. In his opinion, it is perseverance - a necessary quality in order to achieve success. The inventor himself said these words, which we certainly will be able understand the reason for the "fortune" in his life. **"The secret of genius - it is work, perseverance and common sense."** Like Thomas Edison, a lot of other great people have worked hard, persisted in the advancement of their goal and tenaciously committed to the dream that inspired them to action. Therefore, there is nothing surprising to the fact that the names of these men are known to us, and their creations and inventions, are still relevant and being used in our present day.

They did not live the life of fuss and did not allow their thoughts to wander erratically. But they have concentrated their energy, their efforts on the most important things that matters most in life and therefore, invariably succeeded. They drew energy and inspiration in their work, in what they selflessly and devotedly engaged. We all have the same energy and can achieve outstanding success, the only question is: are we willing to pay the necessary price and live by the same principle? If we can answer this question, we will achieve great success and uncommon result in our life time.

So, we are at the end of the fifth chapter of the book called "DISCOVER YOUR SOURCE OF LATENT ENERGY!". We are with you, dear reader, we've crossed the equator: before the end of the book, in remaining five chapters we shall continue to talk to you the resultant consequence of the law of conservation of energy. Namely, that energy never disappears and or reappears, it is only converted from one form to another. In this chapter, we addressed the question of energy reserve. In the next – our study will be focused on the main source of the hidden energy that we need to open in our live. Stay with us!

THE GOLDEN NUGGETS

- We all have incredible strength and size of the latent energy
- Those abilities that we manifest now, are only the tip of the iceberg.
- It is estimated that the average person uses between 3 and 5% of their intellectual energy, and not more than 15% of their physical energy. The rest, of the unused energy remains in reserve
- If we consciously and deliberately concentrate our energy on something, we can achieve all that we want, and achieve outstanding success in any field of activity, which we desire.
- The ability for a high degree of concentration is also called the superior quality of great men
- When we concentrate our focus on some fact, we release energy
- Focus – generates the energy that produces result
- If a person is able to focus, then it is easy to be inspired by the muse
- The more a person can concentrate, the more results he can produce

SELF-EXAMINATION TEST

It should be noted only one answer is required for each question or statement. Next to each answer are marked point. Stacked score will determine the outcome of your training. TEST RESULTS

1. How long can you be focused, to maintain a high degree of concentration?

a. I do not succeed at all - **0 points**

b. For a short time - **1 point**

c. More or less extended period of time - **3 points**

d. As much as you need - **4 points**

2. How hard do you prefer the need to be alone in order to create something substantial?

a. I find it hard to be alone with myself - **0 points**

b. With great difficulty, I can decide on it - **1 point**

c. I like this idea, but it fails with varying degrees of success - **2 points**

d. I find it easy to do it - **4 points**

3. How often do you feel pity for yourself?

a. Sufficient frequency 0 points

b. Sometimes- 1 point

c. Rarely - 3 points

d. Never - 4 point

4. Are you prepared to ensure that in order to achieve your goal, irrespective of any tragic circumstances (for example, the death of loved ones), you will continue to

move toward the goal, not allowing them to stop you?

a. I'm not ready for such a sacrifice! - **0 points**

b. I would like to, but I find it difficult to do so - **1 point**

c. Yes rather than not - **3 points**

d. Definitely, yes! - **4 points**

5. Do you often again and again experience what happened in the past?

a. Sufficient frequency - **0 points**

b. Sometimes - **1 point**

c. Rarely - **3 points**

d. Never - **4 points**

6. How do you manage to block all distractions in your thinking process?

a. It is impossible! - **0 points**

b. Rare - **1 point**

c. Difficulty - **2 points**

d. Always - **4 points**

TEST RESULTS

From 0-8 points - Sorry, you cannot focus on your subject for more or less a long time. You find it hard to focus your attention on one thing, to achieve your goals. This prevents the discovery in their entirety the hidden backup energy that you have. We recommend you do not miss the next chapter of this book, in which you will find answers to your questions.

From 9-18 points - not bad! You're halfway to ensuring that all your backup energy reveal the capabilities of your stored energy. But at the moment, your ability to abandon some interesting and attractive offer in favor of what you really need, is low. The need to develop your endurance, this is necessary to achieve the objective. To achieve this you will find help in this book, when you carefully and diligently apply the various principles stipulated in this book, you will surely achieve the best results.

From 19-24 points - Congratulations, your success in life is guaranteed, you possess the high level of skill to discover and use the backup energy purposes. You can easily focus on your goals and achieve all that you have planned. You are ready to volunteer to go to the limit to get closer to your goal. Do not hesitate at the first instance, to share your skills with others!

PRACTICAL TASKS

1. 1What is responsible for the phenomenal abilities in people with savant syndrome? What are the lessons from this we should learn?

2. We may discover latent energy, through the practice of concentration. How does this happen? How do you intend to practice this principle to release the hidden reserve of energy in your life, to the full potential?

3. Give examples of five great men who have achieved outstanding results. How did they manage to manifest their backup power?

CHAPTER 6:

THE MAIN SOURCE OF ENERGY – WORK

I recall that in the previous chapter, together, dear reader, we examined in detail the question of how to tap into the backup power in our lives. We have seen how the backup energy reserve manifests in people with savant syndrome. We have, in my opinion found the answer to a very important question, namely, what steals our energy? At the conclusion of this chapter we saw that a high degree of concentration - is the best way to unleash our hidden energy reserve. In this chapter, we will focus on the fact that the main instrument of the manifestation of the stored energy is work. These are the critical issues we will be considering, throughout this chapter:

- Work - this is the main way of converting energy
- Work - this is the main energy conversion tool in the finished product
- As a general rule, 10, 000 hours will help you effectively convert your energy.

So, what exactly is the "energy conversion"? CONVERSION (i.e., conversion, transformation) ENERGY COMES THROUGH WORK. Conversion - is a transition from one state to another. [24] **It is through the**

work of a person that energy can be converted on the earth.

Often, young people suffer from the fact that they have an inexpressive, frail figure: slender neck on the narrow shoulders, thin legs that carry the entire body. The impression is that the wind will blow them off. Such people are referred to as, "skinny bones". This kind of young people always arouse pity; this automatically prevents others from taking them serious. Fragile appearance makes them even at 28 years to be placed in the "Boys" category. How many young people lose the traction and do nothing with regard to their shape and their appearance!

When I was about 19 years, I looked just as unintelligible and completely undignified and it hurt my feelings. I wanted to look authoritative and solid. I thought that a man should not look like this. I was sure that every self-respecting man should have a credible appearance: pumped up torso, broad shoulders, strong arms to embrace his wife, always feel safe and like a stone wall. But we were not born with this kind of unique feature. I went to the gym with a very clear intention to do everything I could do to make my appearance become more robust to command more respect. The same may make any overly skinny guy, and after a while, experience a dramatic change in his body, his biceps become inflated, it no longer looked like a goner from the camp, but he now looked good in the mirror, as his muscle gains shape and topography. What happened to the guy? How did his body undergo such wonderful changes? He was not operated upon, so as to join the muscle? What happened to him? **The required energy has always been**

in the man, but have now been transformed it into a product. Thanks to its efforts at the gym, thanks to the virtue of work, a man found the hidden energy and turned it into a desired product - a beautiful shaped body. Transformation of energy! After all, the energy does not appear out of nowhere and disappear without a trace, it can only be modified. Or, take the opposite example: the person is overweight, and it is clear that on its own the weight will not just disappear, you need to spend energy in order to lose weight. Again, it requires work. Where goes the extra weight when a person loses weight? After all, the weight was not removed surgically. But, weight was lost, it is the result of energy conversion, energy simply evolved. And let someone complains that he cannot lose weight: it is impossible to tell ...! Who's supposed to do the loosing of the weight? It all depends on labor! And between the modifications of energy is one word: WORK. Manifesting the energy or not, the only one thing that makes the difference is- the effort through work that has been done. If nothing happens, then the answer is simple: work have not been done. WORK IS THE ONLY TOOL THAT REVEALS THE FORCE HIDDEN OF OUR ENERGY.

WORK – THE MAIN TOOL OF ENERGY CONVERTION

Work - this is the most basic way to exhaustion and energy conversion. For example, when a person goes to work and perform his necessary activity, his labor is converted into a salary in the form of money, through which his livelihood is enhanced: he is able to buy food, clothes, pay for utilities and travel on public transport.

These funds allow the person to continue his physical existence and not starve. Although at work, he does not on his own print the banknotes on the machine and mint the coins. He's only doing something, what society needs: producing goods or offering services, creating wealth and generating creative ideas and in the form of books, articles, research, lectures, etc. But time, energy and effort is spent by the person at work, this returns to him at the end of the month, only this time in a modified state - in the form of cash.

Another example: the artist sits in front of a canvas for 16-20 hours. It is not unusual canvas - canvas as in canvas, like any other artist he uses his paint and brush of the canvas. But in the end, it turns out unique, in its characteristics, an image that will not be confused with anything else. For some of these canvases with paint applied to them, people pay millions of dollars to acquire. What makes a painting a masterpiece? The special artist has worked hard, the result of his hard work is an expensive product? He is engaged in creative work, in which his creative energy is converted into a beautiful picture.

Or when learning, a specific time is invested in a given specific discipline. During this time, the energy contained in this knowledge is converted to yourself. The knowledge is no longer abstract, they become clear to you, the more you go through detailed study on the given subject, the more you become a professional or a specialist in that given field. The acquired knowledge, increased the volume of your personality. The same thing happens when you meditate on God's Word, if you are reading about the faith, the spirit of faith comes upon you – it will make you grow wings behind your back, you will believe that everything is possible, because you will be under the influence of the power of the impacted knowledge; If you read about the power, then, accordingly, you are filled with power, energy and effectivity - you know in whatever venture you undertake, that, you will certainly succeed! What did you do? You converted the power of God, which is contained in His word, and it becomes a mass inside you. Thanks to work, you converted the word of God in the area strength and power into your life.

If you hear any word of the wise, and do not find the time to work on it on your own, it is as if you did not hear anything at all. ANY NECESSARY INFORMATION YOU HEAR IS TRANSFORMED THROUGH EFFORTS AND WORK IN VOLUME, BEFORE IT CAN BECOME MASS INSIDE YOU. If you do not do this, then it would be like putting the water in the freezer for 1 minute, and you think that during this time it would have formed an ice, *"But the water was in the freezer? Why did it not turn to ice?"*. it did not have enough time for its transformation, the qualitative transition from one state to another. So we sometimes flippantly declare, having barely heard something: *"Ah! I already knew about it!"*- Although, in fact, we just fleetingly heard about it, with little or no understanding of what we heard. It's a principle that, those things you have not labored on, YOU DO NOT KNOW!

It will not be yours, unless you take the time to feel the heat, dive, get to the core and understand the speech, one might stay, at the genetic level!

Criminologists and the graphologists engaged in the study of human handwriting. Their interest is explained by the fact that the handwriting, almost unmistakably identifies the author of the note. After all, everyone has a unique style of writing, which is formed during that time - the school children's, training elements of the letters with the help of formulations, produce in their writing skills. The handwriting of each person is individual, despite the fact that when writing people do not invent anything new, it somehow stands out – we all write the same letter of the native alphabet, which are not more than fifty. The synchronization of the mind function, the nerves and the body helps to carve out the distinctive script style of that person.

This phenomenon explains the teachings of Pavlov, according to him the letters formed skill almost never changed, a foothold in the higher nervous system in the form of a dynamic stereotype. The way a person performs all the curls and angles in writing, is deposited in his mind, absorbed in his flesh and blood. Those are things that, the person begins to fulfill on a subconscious level - roughly speaking, it assimilates and makes it "his". Even if a person tries to change his own style, and start to write with the other hand, what he says usually helps expert to easily determine the author's writing [25].

Similarly, as you shape the uniqueness of your hand-writing, constantly repeating the same movements when writing manuscripts, having to build and lay inward, then only as a result of repetitive actions, a permanent way return to the material, teaching, word, that information are put in their subconscious. It is by working on ourselves that we achieve a noticeable and tangible success.

Or remember how we master the skill of using a tennis racket or playing a soccer ball? Any person who is professionally engages in sports, for 2-3 hours a day honing blows or supply, confirm this. When a beginner tennis player only picks up a racket, all his attention is accented on how he holds the racket. But then, through constant practice, the ability to hold the racket in his hands turns into a habit, the athlete ceases to control this process, and this is gone into his subconscious level. Elementary movement is automatic in man, he unconsciously takes 3-4 steps forward, like a real player. Therefore, with increasing skill when a tennis player pitches, he is more likely to determine where the ball will land, and then he calculates where to move, to hit it smartly, ensuring himself the better chance of winning.

The same thing happens when you begin to work on yourself, building yourself through self-education and those daily routines that help you to move towards the goal. When we " do a thorough investigation or research " by applying ourselves to the demand of loads of reading and studies, when we make our regular classes, with time, it enters into our flesh and blood, our subconscious level, we begin to live this. We just cannot imagine without this more than life! We do not want to waste our time trying to sit in front of the TV for hours or chat with someone on the phone. These daily activities increases in us, it makes us to experience the change: the change in our character, our outlook on life, our thinking and judgment. We become changed from the person were before. In this way, the energy is converted into a qualitatively new state.

When we are consistent in our efforts and we invest time into it, we increase the volume of our personality, which allows, in turn, the ability to determine our lives in advance, to develop a program of constructive steps, that will surely lead us to the desired goal. Personally to me it allows me to see and plan my life 300-500 years in advance, I can see what's left after me even when I will no longer be on earth.

When one looks ahead, he ceases to live in yesterday, he begins to see not only what is under his feet, and much more. He can plan his life; he sees the path that lies before him. And it's an exciting experience when passing a certain segment of the path, having lived a certain period of his life, a person sees how to implement what he had planned yesterday and fulfills what he carefully calculates.

WORK - THE MAIN INSTRU-MENT OF PRODUCTION

Any work- it is a process of energy storage, which over time gives a certain product. In other words: work – this is the main tool of transformation of energy, which we all have, in the finished product. This is the same as in minerals: they are always in the rock, but their useful qualities are detected and are released only when they are extracted from the earth and are converted into a product that the person needs. Diamonds or oil are already present in the ground, but only through the production process can it be recovered and used to benefit us. Only through the work done on them by cleaning and processing, that we get the value that is actually present. But it is impossible to easily release the wealth, hidden in the bowels of the earth without work.

Or, for example, I want to write a book. The Idea is there in the head, but no one sees it. How do I release all my great ideas? Only through hard work! All my most brilliant ideas and fantasies and dreams will remain hidden as long as I do not start the production process, and not put efforts and begin to work on it, in order to transfer them from the idea in the mind to a tangible material in form of a book. Who would have known about the greatness of the gift of these writers Leo Tolstoy and Fyodor Dostoyevsky, if they had left all their good thoughts in their heads, not bothering to even somehow express them on paper? So, for a person to increase the muscle, or to lose weight – work is needed, to write the book and before it can be published - again, needs work. Whatever you do: to build a house, or build factories, construct planes, or ships, create new varieties of tea, or meditate, think, acquire knowledge – whatever the case may be, ENERGY IS ONLY CONVERTED TO THE PRODUCT THROUGH LABOR!

Work - this is the only way in which energy is converted into any material product. In a formula it would look like this: KNOWLEDGE + SKILLS + EFFORT = WORK = PRODUCT.

Easily all of the above will be a useless burden. To get real results, real product, it needs necessary action. For many people, this knowledge remains only as information in their head. They lack their application in practice. But smart people acquire knowledge endeavor, add labor, then transformed knowledge into skills, and they get the finished product.

Please note, at what stage of efforts: does transition from knowledge to understanding occurs. Efforts are required intelligence to see the full picture and the details of what needs to be done. In order to simply know what to do, you need intelligence, you need to organize the production process - to build a chain of necessary actions that will lead you to the desired result. And above all, it must be seen. **That work - is always something that comes after understanding.**

And here is the wisdom needed – the know-how and in what order to act. The process begins with the fact that a person sees a picture of a fully finished product - sees the color from the mind, from A to Z, noticing all the minutest details. And then to getting to the final stage -Getting the product released - needs work.

Let us illustrate, I offer the following explanation. People say: *"without effort you cannot easily pull the fish from the pond."* That is, the fish is in the pond, the fact that it exists in nature, does not have any impact on your life, in principle: your table is empty, and will remain so, your stomach is empty, hungry and rumbling from starvation. But to lay the table, and for you to satisfy yourself and satisfy your hunger for deliciously cooked fish, you need to go through the production process - work. First, you need to catch a fish, to know what kind of bait to get, what type of equipment you need, to get the job done.

You have to be an excellent fisherman and with a lot of patience, because fish do not bite on your hook just because you deigned to come to the pond. If you succeed with this, and take the catch home, it is necessary to know how to clean the fish, because of the scales – necessary work needs to be done to clean the fish, in addition, it is important not mess up the preparation of fish, in order words to not undercook the fish. Undone fish are not free from parasites and microbes- rest assured! – This can have adverse effect on your life, if it does, as a result of your thoughtlessness or carelessness, gets into your stomach. That is, before you sit down, you have to roll up our sleeves and work hard to eat a great meal of fish.

HOW THE "RULE OF 10 000 HOURS" WILL HELP YOU TO EFFECTIVELY CONVERT YOUR ENERGY?

If I were asked what should be given to people most of the time, I would have said - training. Train more than sleep. No matter what goal you pursue, you will not regret, if you follow this strict rule. People, in fact, are capable of infinite improvement and achievement. Success depends on purpose and diligence.

- **Mas Oyama (1923—1994), a martial arts master, the founder of Kyokushin Karate style.**

Thus, WORK - a major source of ENERGY CONVERSION. Then the logical question arises: how much time is necessary to devote to work? How much time is necessary for work, to succeed, for energy conversion is to occur at such a level that it is impossible to ignore? In answering this question, Mas Oyama said that "training" - that is, labor, improvement of skills in the chosen direction of activity - people should devote most of their time to it. This time should exceed the amount of time that person devotes to sleep. We sleep about 8 hours a day. Thus, the time that we need to spend to successfully convert our energy into a ready-to-eat product should occupy our schedule more than a third of our day. This is forms the point of view of the martial arts founder of Kyokushin Karate style.

How much it is necessary to answer this question, I will say that you need to work to devote so much time! To succeed, you have to work as long as necessary! **The more you work, to build your inner "Self", the better for you, the greater your results and efficiency will be.** THE LONGER YOU WORK, THE GREATER THE EFFECT OF YOUR EFFORTS.

Where are the outstanding achievements? Are they by chance or by adhering to rule or procedures? Who are they - the people who achieve outstanding results - lucky to get, lucky by the tail, or those who are consciously preparing for an encounter with the opportunities through the direct investment of their time and efforts? Malcolm Gladwell (1963 p.), Canadian journalist and popular sociologist, in his book "Geniuses and outsiders," states that **geniuses are not born but are a result of the hard training you love** [11]. There is a pattern by which the convertible energy can bring you great result. You want to know how it works? I invite you, dear reader, to get acquainted with the principle, which is convention-ally called the 10, 000 hours Rule.

Decades ago the psychologist Anders Ericsson, together with two colleagues, conducted a study in the Academy of Music in Berlin. The survey was conducted among students of violin, they were divided into three groups: the first includes the star and potential soloists of world-class level, second - those who are evaluated as promising musicians and the third - the students from department of music education, who, at best, have a "chance" to become teachers at music school. All participants were asked the same question: how many hours have they all practiced since they first picked up the violin, to this day?

The starting conditions were the same for all students: almost all of them started to play music at the same age —when they were about five years. At first, between them there was no difference: for the first few years, they all dedicated about two to three hours a week, to music studies. Then, by eight years, the differences became apparent. Those who subsequently turned out to be better, exercised more than any other: for nine years in their "working" time was six hours a week, at twelve years it was between - eight to fourteen - sixteen. It was not until twenty years, when they have become focused and concentrated that their skills improved, giving music lessons in more than thirty hours a week. As a result, a 20-year milestone behind in the best students, were up to 10 000 hours of training, while in baggage "middling" - about 8000, and the "outsiders" - the future teachers of music - not more than 4,000.

The researchers **did not find a single person who have achieved a high level of skill, not putting much effort or exercising less than their peers.** It can be concluded that respondents differed from each other only by how hard they worked. And they do not just work harder than everyone else, they worked much more. It is from this conclusion on the results to which they have come with time: someone was shining a spot as music teacher in secondary school, and someone else waiting for the world stage. And there was no justification for why each of these young people was at the place, where they resided at the time of the study.

In the same way, and you, dear reader, there is no reason to wonder why one gets everything and the other (and possibly you) - nothing. Everything in this life is subject to the laws and principles, nothing is accidental: if you work, you will succeed, if refuse to "plow", your destiny – will be in the middle, or among the laggards in the "tail". The only way to achieve a high level of skill, life or income is only through hard work, putting in a lot of effort. It is impossible to reach the level of masterly possession of anything without exerting a degree of force through labor and not breaking a sweat during your attempts.

In his book, Gladwell quotes neurologist Daniel Levitin, who made the following conclusion from the facts obtained: *"The emerging picture from such studies is that 10,000 hours of practice is required to achieve the level of mastery associated with being a world class expert-in anything. In studies after studies, of composers, basketball players, fiction writers, ice skaters, concert pianists, chess players, master criminals, and what have you, this number comes up again and again... no one has yet found a case in which true world-class was accomplished in less time. It seems that it takes the brain this long to assimilate all that it needs to know to achieve true mastery. "[11].* It is agreed that to achieve excellence in any activities, it is impossible without a long-term practice.

Actor Michael Masterson, regardless of the Gladwell findings also concluded that 10,000 hours of practice – breaking this milestone, that person becomes outstanding (virtuoso) in the business. Based on his observations, he concluded that there are four levels of ownership in some skill: incompetence, competence, skillful and virtuosity. As part of his concept, Michael argues as follows: *"To overcome incompetence, you have practiced about 1000 hours in the area you selected.*

To achieve excellence, you need to continue training and to bring the total to 5,000 hours. Virtuosity is rare. You cannot reach it, just practicing. You will also need natural talent, but even in this case, the training will take at least 10 thousand hours." Although Michael Masterson graduation differ from the calculations of Malcolm Gladwell, in the end, they agree on one thing: the magic number, leading to mastery, which is derived by the scientific method - it is 10 000 hours of preparation.

So, what do we need to convert our latent energy to a high level of skill? Work! If you still do not know the English language, all you just need is to start work - to study the language for a certain amount of time, and then the conversion will happen, there will be energy in the form of knowledge. What I did not know yesterday, I begin to understand, I begin to speak - and start doing what I could not do before! But the energy, the ability to learn a foreign language has always been with me. Thus, **the energy is always available to you, you need only to determine how and on what you'll expend it on.**

This is the end of the sixth chapter which is devoted to the work as the main source of our energy. Throughout this chapter we have analyzed that work– is not only the main way of converting energy, but also the main instrument of the transformation of energy into a finished product. I think that the section devoted to the way in which Rule 10 000 hours is applied, can help us to more efficiently convert our energy. This is very important, and you can use this knowledge in practice, by applying it directly to your life, and thus in the process you change yourself and the people around you, for the better. In the next chapter we will focus on self-restraint as the main source of our energy. We will look at this topic in a most detailed way. Please consider the following questions:

- Why can't I not afford to relax?
- What can be opposed to comfort and laziness?
- How can restrictions help me release the latent energy?

See you in the next chapter!

THE GOLDEN NUGGETS

- Only work reveals the hidden power within us
- Work - is the main tool of transformation of energy, which we all have, resulting in a finished product
- Energy is converted into a product only through labor
- Work - this is the only way in which energy is converted into any material product
- Work - this is the most basic way to exhaustion, energy conversion
- If you hear any word of the wise, and do not find the time to work on it on your own, it is as if you did not hear anything at all
- The information you receive is necessary, to transform the way work is done and effort in volume.
- There is not one person who would have achieved a high level of skill, without putting too much effort or exercising less than his peers.
- Geniuses are not born but are a result of hard training you love
- If you are one of those who knows how to "work hard" and "plow" struggling, it is impossible for you not to get ahead
- Energy is always available to you; you need only to determine how and on what you will use it

SELF-EXAMINATION TEST

It should be noted only one answer is necessary for each question or statement. Next to each answer are marked point. Stacked score will determine the outcome of your training.

1.   Are you doing well then, what do you do?

a.   From the work, horses die! - **0 points**

b.   To be honest, I do everything carelessly - **1 point**

c.   I try to be guided by this principle in my live, but it does not always apply - **3 points**

d.   My principle: to be the best in everything and whatever I undertake - **4 points**

2.   Whether the statement is true for you: "I always do more than is required of me?"

a.   In no way - **0 points**

b.   Partly - **1 point**

c.   To a greater degree- **3 points**

d.   My credo: "Not a day without extra mile" - **4 points**

3.   Is it fair to have this statement? "I think that perseverance in me more than capable"

a.   I do not agree with it - **0 points**

b.   This is true in part - **1 points**

c.   I am very persistent person - **3 points**

d.   Perseverance - my strengths. I always pursue all my projects to the end no matter what - **4 points**

4. Are you working on yourself?

a. What is it, work on myself? - **0 points**

b. I'm too lazy for it - **1 point**

c. Every time I start enthusiastically engaging in the process, but then my zeal fades, and as a result I lack power for continuity - **2 points**

d. I do it continuously and purposefully - **4 points**

TEST RESULTS

From 0-2 points - sorry, you have a high degree of laziness, therefore, most likely, you do not even know what it means to really work. It does not allow you to successfully convert the energy in you. You lack the diligence and persistence in the selected case. However, do not worry, there is always a way out: use the lessons contained in this book, and then the results you get will please you.

From 3-7 points - sorry, your ability to convert energy into useful actions, and products are not at a high level. You underestimate the role of diligence and permanent actions that are capable of performing miracles, if directed in the right direction. However, you can improve your ability to: complete the practical exercises at the end of each chapter of this book, and you will be able to reach a new level of disclosure of the potential energy contained in you.

From 8-12 points – am happy for you! You have a good potential to convert the energy that you have, into a good quality product, for that you are quite functional and diligent. It is necessary to work on them to improve these indicators and become more efficient. This this book is designed to help you, read it very carefully to the end, and you will learn a lot of interesting and useful principles that will help you along the way.

From 13-16 points - You have a wonderful result! Apparently, you can be called a recognized expert on the ability to convert his energy into a high quality product. Perhaps you are the one person who has virtually failed to disclose in its entirety its latent energy. If so, share your skills with others!

PRACTICAL TASKS

1. What is work and how does work help reveal hidden sources of energy in you? How does this principle affect you and how do you intend to apply it into your life?

2. Please comment on the statement by M. Gladwell: "Geniuses are not born but are a result of hard training you love." What does this mean for you? What lessons did you draw from these words?

CHAPTER 7:

SELF-RESTRAINT - A MAIN SOURCE OF ENERGY

So, dear reader, we are progressing with our study on "DISCOVER YOUR SOURCE OF LATENT ENERGY". In this book, we talk to you about energy and the most important principle, which reveals the energy that exists around us, is as follows: the energy does not disappear without a trace, and does not come out of nothing, the total energy of an isolated system remains constant- it is said to be conserved over time. Energy can neither be created nor destroyed: rather, it is transformed from one form to another. This law of conservation of energy, which is known to us from school, but I think that with this book you, dear reader, you will discover the principles that you are not taught in school.

In the preceding chapter, we examined in details, that work - is not only the main way of converting energy, but also the main instrument of the transformation of energy into a finished product. In this chapter, we will focus on self-restraint as the fundamental source of our energy. We are going to be considering the following questions:

- Why can we not afford to relax?
- What can be opposed to comfort and laziness?
- How can limitations help us release the latent energy?

WHY YOU CAN NOT AFFORD TO RELAX?

Lazy man in dishonorable piece is similar to a fixed wading in water, which, in addition to the stench and despicable vermin, produces nothing.

- MV Lomonosov (1711-1765), the first Russian scientist-naturalist of world importance, lexicographer, chemist and physicist

So, we found that any form of work is designed to convert energy into visible product. We talked about work- this is the way by which all invisible ideas or energies are released into the visible world. That is why **we must always be in the process of work and cannot afford to relax because when there is a relaxation there is energy loss.**

In the US, there was a trend that people will likely become millionaires Americans in the first generation - these were more than 80% of their total number. [26] Such people lived poorly, but they wanted to live well, and therefore sort to escape poverty. They were not inclined to spend much on prestigious products as much as the Native Americans who are originally born in this prosperous country, who are in a comfort zone.

Those who are not in straitened circumstances, and is not easy to deny themselves and to lose, at least a minimum level of comfort. This in turn is what becomes destructive to them: Native Americans succeed less and are less likely to achieve outstanding results than the newcomers. The same pattern can be observed in large cities, which attracts provincials: as a rule, they are more penetrative than the indigenous residents of the capital. They will stand on their feet, to acquire the apartment and a car, have a successful business. Because life itself is forcing them to look for opportunities to happen, and for them to catch it at the first possible instance.

Those who were "lucky" to have an apartment in the capital, inherited from parents, and having stable life, there is no need to take risks and are not desperately looking for a way out of any situation: their life is quite sized, predictable and comfortable. But this plays a cruel joke on this people: when the "upstart" newcomers occupy all top positions, the indigenous population begins to mutter irritably. And the only difference between these people is that some, due to the lack of that experience, mobilized and are always ready to rush into battle, they are full of energy and strength. And others, due to the presence of complacency and comfort - have allowed themselves to relax, and thereby not taking advantage of the opportunities that life present. They are adversely affected because of their complacent attitude towards life.

We begin with, you should be aware that we already have all the features of the Creator.

With such wealth, they continue to be losers, no manifestations in life, nothing is achieved and no tangible impact in life – they make attempts to find justification for their own laziness. Nothing makes something impossible, as laziness, as a high level of comfort and selfishness. All of these things "kill" the energy, dissipate it without leaving a single gram on creative and constructive things.

Therefore, comfort, tranquility, laziness, complacency - is a manifestation of the largest form of self-hatred, the greatest punishment, curse, with which you can reward yourself. And no matter the kind of laziness in question, be it: mental, physical, spiritual - if entertained, you will never be able to create anything. YOU SHOULD NOT LET YOURSELF TO RELAX, BECAUSE LAZINESS AND HIGH LEVEL OF COMFORT LEADS TO LOSS OF ENERGY.

We all have the power, that is energy. And if they do not appear, then this is the explanation

Comfort as disability, limits our ability to achieve outstanding success, and the ability to convert into visible physical world, our ideas and dreams. Almost all people in this world crave comfort and do everything to ensure that their life becomes cozy and comfortable. Statistics also show that comfort for a man - it's death, this is what is killing us, selfishness and lust only meet their needs and desires at the heart of the love for comfort.

Ephraim Dictionary interprets the meaning of the word "comfort" as: 1. The set of amenities. 2. The state of inner satisfaction which arises under the influence of any favorable conditions, circumstances, etc. [27]. This means that if a person lives in comfort, he is completely surrounded by amenities, favorable circumstances and conditions. Comfort - a sense of security, stability and the state of carelessness, the confidence that everything is going well, a sense of peace and tranquility that lasts for too long.

When a person is in a comfortable environment, he does not have the urge to change anything, he does not want to improve and evolve, this in turn leads to more degradation. That is why the comfortable life for the people - is death, it is the inhibition of individual development, it is a disability. The person who really loves himself and wants to imagine the good, should consciously and independently get out the comfort zone: constantly evolving, looking for new challenges, meeting them, working tirelessly and hereby realizing his goals and plans, reaching greater and greater heights in his professional activities and service to humanity.

Comfort should never become an end in itself for us, because, the moment comfort is reached, then begins the process of human degradation. Where there is too much rest, stagnation begins, life turns into a swamp, which soon begins to stink. Comfort is similar to stagnant swampy water, which, in the apt words of Lomonosov, is not able to produce anything sensible *"apart from the stench and despicable vermin."*

When I was thirty years old, I did not have a car. I could not afford it. Like many other people, I traveled by public transport and did a lot of walking. Thanks to the constant physical exertion, I was always smart and in good physical shape. It looked just fine.

Time passed, and I bought a car. I spend most of the time sitting, and, to my great regret, I was no more in a good bodily shape like I used to be. Now I have to devote to my hard scheduled time to engage in exercise at the gym, to maintain my fitness, but before I was perfectly fit without necessarily working out at the gym. From morning till night, by moving on foot and with public transport, I was able to have a physical activity without undue costs necessary, maintaining a slim and fit stature. That is, comfort gave me a disservice! And we often crave comfort, striving to ensure that everything in our live come easily and effortlessly. We should not seek to have comfort, because life in comfort is somewhat destructive. In the physical world without a proper load, muscles weaken and degenerate, the heart ceases to pump blood with the necessary intensity. The same thing can happen to us if we allow ourselves to relax - at first for a moment, and then – as the days go by and clock starts ticking. As much as it may be uncomfortable, exercise does not allow stagnant blood in our veins, just overcoming obstacles helps us to keep fit: to be fit, lean and therefore we maintain a healthy physique and life. By leaving the comfort zone, we actually do ourselves lots of good, it gives us happiness, brings fullness of life decision. Problems no matter how difficult they may seem, strengthens us and shakes our inner "muscles". We become more though, strengthened and resilient. **Discomfort helps you to grow.**

WHAT COULD BE AGAINST COMFORT AND PLEASURE?

The best antidote to feelings of comfort and complacency are crisis and problems. This is when things start to go wrong, as we have assumed, when breaking down the usual reaction for us, patterns of behavior or conduct of business. Usually, problems and crisis makes a man come out of the misleading state of equilibrium, stability and peace. And, often, it is in crisis that is the starting point of his brilliant ascent to the top.

When he was 9 years old, he was expelled from school.

At age 17, he was expelled from the college.

He was forced to sleep on the floor, he had to buy food, take the bottle. In order to eat properly, every Sunday he would walked 7 miles to the Hare Krishna temple.

At the age of 20 in search of "enlightenment", he went to India, but in the end, turned out to be almost on the verge of death due to the severe climate of that country.

At 21, he established his company for the production of personal computers, the office   was located in a garage. He sold all that he had and invested it in the business in order to save the startup capital.

Starting wasn't that very smooth, it was difficult for the company to make any tangible head way, and his partner left because he lacked faith in the business, he could not imagine any pathway to the success of their business.

Creating a new computer with a different operating system, make it difficult for him to find suit-

able investors into his project, all attempt by him to breakthrough the company of personal computer was cumbersome and success seem very elusive. He was tenaciously committed to his dream against all odds, the discomfort he went through toughened him, this brought out his creative genius.

At age 25, he was able to break through the hard soil, he managed to get an investor to finance his project, this personal computer became an outstanding success, that exceeded all expectations in personal computing industry. The young man suddenly became one of the richest men in America. The name of this person - Steve Jobs. His life was loaded with all sorts of crises, which did not allow him to relax for a minute. Perhaps precisely because of this, he was able to go from failure to becoming a successful billionaire. Though it was hard and uncomfortable, the benefits of the presence of problems and crises - was obvious. In the words of positive psychologist Robert Biswas-Diener, author and instructor at Portland State University, *"Distress tolerance is important [...] because it allows you to become stronger, wiser, mentally agile, and most important, happier in a more resilient, and therefore durable, way."*

Bill Gates (1955 p.), An American entrepreneur and social activist, philanthropist, one of the founders and former largest shareholder to Microsoft, says that *"success does not teach anything, it only convinces the intelligent people that they cannot lose".*

Sometimes it is helpful to lose comfort, to survive the crisis and to experience the problem, rather than relax by the fact that everything is comfortable. The latter offers you less help in challenging you to discovering your hidden energy and potentials. Crisis, inconvenience and hardship, what we call the discomfort of life are the best thing that helps us in every situation. Do not wait for the crisis to propel you to become successful or activate the release of the "dormant" hidden energies in you. Become proactive. Make yourself get out of your comfort zone by artificially, consciously and willingly putting yourself in uncomfortable situations, from where you discover the new capabilities, thereby "squeezing" out, your hidden potential. To find a backup energy is possible through this form of restriction.

"Limit" - it means inconveniencing oneself from any known limits, terms and conditions, by putting in some frames, and boundaries. For example, it is appropriate to introduce restrictions for yourself in area of your spending. Very often you can hear from people that they do not know how to save money and they seem to be happy in doing that, but here's the problem - it is impossible to have a balanced financial life with this pattern of behavior without any form of restriction on your personal spending. The inability to deny ourselves and to limit the expenditure leads to the fact that from time to time, that, we will always lack money. Probably many are familiar with this expression, *"Money, like water running out through your fingers,"* – As this is true about people, that without some financial discipline, there can't be financial sufficiency, the same is applicable with the energy in us. And with energy: when a person does not know how to put some restraint on himself and he keep running out of energy gas.

The benefits of limitations and its scope of influence:

- We are able to stimulate growth
- push for action
- it makes you think
- increases our capacity
- disciplines your life
- disrupt the comfort zone, because comfort - this is what is convenient to us, might be that which is exactly what is devastating for us.
- release the spare time to get closer to success, and time - is the most important resource of our life.
- create a border, not allowing us to stray off course, it pulls us over, thereby creating a road map for us reaching our goal
- and it contributes to increase

HOW SELF-RESTRAINT HELPS RELEASE LATENT ENERGY?

A bottle of beer in the morning - this is a step into the unknown.
- Nikolay Fomenko (1962 p.), Soviet and Russian musician, actor, radio and TV presenter, sports commentator and columnist, showman, Honored Artist of Russia

If you restrain yourself - in food, in pleasure, enter-tainment - then you gain energy. Believers of many religions practice of fasting - abstaining from food. Because when a person eats, he expends energy, and at the same time, when he denies himself some food, then stores it. By denying yourself food, physical energy is converted to spiritual energy. Restrictions on food give man power in the spirit: it makes the spirit become more alert, sharper and brighter to see - this is the result of energy conversion. Even Jesus Christ, the Son of God, said it was necessary to pray and fast, because he knew the law on ground: that nothing can be released without labor. He needed to work in the spirit, to make spiritual work. It was only through the work he could draw energy, so that even for Him there was no exception.

When a person does not smoke, does not drink, does not talk, he is at all times remains focused, sober. What makes this happen? The reason is that his energy is not dissipated, he has unbroken focus on his goals! But when a person smokes or drinks, he is wasting his energy on empty things, he dispels energy or squanders his energy. The result is that there is no focus, no coordination, he cannot harness his energy to achieve the desired goal. In energy conversion: if a person spent it on an empty pursuit, that energy is wasted and lost, the ability to achieve set goals is deterred, because the energy necessary to succeed is emaciated.

If you put restriction on yourself in some areas of life, the energy you have left is reserved, and this reserved energy will be enough to achieve the goals that you set yourself. When you are focused, you are full of energy!

With purpose, engage in periodical fasting, try to limit yourself by refusing to lead a hectic life. Because in this case, you accumulate energy, converting it and directing it into other, more important to useful things.

For example, athletes before the competition limit themselves in the area of sexual relationships, precisely because they are not in sport for fun and they are there for this important reason, to win, and for the sake of achieving this victory, they are willing to pay the price – put a limit on themselves in sexual terms.

It is known that a great boxer Rocky Marciano refrained from sexual relations with his wife for a few months before fights. He was the only heavy-weight boxer, who retired undefeated. Abstinence tradition is still strong in energy demanding sports such as boxing. Many modern fighters such as Oscar De La Hoya and Manny Pacquiao's refuse to engage in sex before a fight. Proponents of this belief think that the male athlete loses its vitality whenever he ejaculates [28].

An experienced psychologist-practitioner, master of psychology, author of several books on traditional systems of healing, Roman Sedykh specialist, answering the question of how productive is the prohibition on sex before the game, says: *"The prohibition of sex before the match in most cases are completely justified. In addition, sex makes the man to relax, because testosterone is emitted from the man during orgasm, this hormone is not only responsible for sex, but also the ambition and male aggressiveness neces-sary for fighting. A man, on the contrary after sex, is extremely relaxed."[29].* This is very important because athletes want to be full of energy and not spend it on comfort. They want to direct their energies in the right direction- towards the game and convert it into victory. If you are an ambitious person, you will care about the outcome of the battle, you will not be still, win or lose your team, you were clearly satisfied with just winning outcome of the match. And for this, you will be ready to limit yourself to preserve and increase the energy that will help you win!

This wonderful film tells the story "Legend № 17" - the best Russian film in 2013 based on real events and tells of the rise to fame of the Soviet hockey player Valeri Kharlamov.

Early in his hockey career the famous hockey player with his friend Alexander Gusev played for the local team in the Ural town of Chebarkul. The situation at the provincial team did not fit into the ambitious plans of the rising stars of Soviet sport. Hockey players did not show any eagerness to win, they are guided by the desire to hold a place among the "middling" – somewhere in the middle of the standings. When asked why they are satisfied with the status quo, why they did not play at full strength, and agree to the match-fixing, their response to the questions was a big burden to the players that were playing with all their abilities. To increase their standings, performance and getting better result will mean the team will have to go extra mile, stretch themselves a little further and work harder, this was demanded by Kharlamov, but not a member of the team showed any interest at his demands.

To make things worse, their regular habit was to party during matches, and in the process they took different women to bed. It would seem to them that they are living an elegant life of fame, honor, covered tables. That girls were at their service at any time – gives them a false sense of joy! But Khar-lamov was unhappy. Waking up one day, after a night in the arms of an unknown girl, and struggling with a hangover, Kharlamov woke his friend, Valery Gusev, up, and forced him to go for a jog. Desperate Kharlamov forced his companion to climb one of the towers of the power plants and the metal cable, with the hands to move to the next tower. When they reached the middle and hanging at a great height above the city, Kharlamov turned to his friend:

- Gus, and what are your plans? Are you still thinking about CSKA, about the team? To one-day play with the Canadians? See the world?

- Che, do you want right here to talk about it?

- We do not have any prospects, we waste, we have thrown in the trash - you and me - as trash, you know? Because of this, 10 years of training because of this all our dream – are in shambles!

-Better Die than play "dry" and kowtow to all sorts of goats! Do you want to live? DO YOU WANT TO LIVE? !!

- Yes!!!

- So let's move, Gus, let's move! Come on ...

Even if this is an act in this movie, and in reality it did not happen, we, the audience, through the discourse by the actors we are motivated to think. After all, this could well be the case, if not in the life of Kharlamov, this can be the case in the life of any other ambitious young men. The legend of Soviet sport at number 17 knew very well that in order not to lose shape and be ever out of a provincial Chebarkul team, you need to stop living like everyone lived. To be in the USSR national team and work with Tarasov, it will be impossible for them to play and train at full capacity, by spending time in restaurants, in company with strange girls, giving themselves to drinking liquor.

Valeri Kharlamov was well aware that the energy of their youth cannot to be spent on things that only brings them momentary satisfaction, that they have to focus their energy on the real game of hockey. Apparently, he was in agreement with Nikolay Fomenko, whose words you read in the beginning of this section: "A bottle of beer in the morning - this is a step into the unknown." Kharlamov did not want to walk in the dark, on the contrary, he wanted to go in the opposite direction, so he had to give up comfort. When we allow ourselves to relax, we waste our energy and head for the "unknown".

Strong man – is not the one who can get a lot, but the one who can give up a lot of things.

ALL MEN WHO BECAME GREAT, THANKS TO THE FRAMEWORK, THAT THEY SET THEIR OWN RULES. Great people - those who have learned to put their own limits and limitations. Create a self-frame - this is the greatest gift that you can give yourself! After all, restrictions - is the wisest virtue, that a person can choose for himself.

Self-limiting - it is one of the methods of energy production:

- When others are sleeping, you work
- When others walk and roam around, you work
- When others eat, you refrain
- When others are laughing, you meditate and pray at this time
- When the others play "the fool", you are reading

Restrictions do not allow us to dissipate energy, but helps us to store it in order to achieve the main thing in life, it helps us not to be distracted by minor things of the moment. It is through self-restraint; you can uncover a hidden energy sources that make you able to enrich the people around you. When a person is randomly consuming his energy, wasting it on major and minor things indiscriminately, irrespective of their priority and importance, he can for example, only have enough for the full year, to sew only one suit. While someone else, due to the restrictions, may be able to sew about 5000 suit at the same length of period. Regulations that you bring into your life consciously and voluntarily, allows you to store energy of incredible amount: at a time when others have scattered their energy and spent it on vain stuffs, you accumulate it.

So, throughout this chapter we have examined in detail, that the self-restraint or call it circumscription - this is the main source of preserving our energy. We found out why we should not allow ourselves to relax, and this can be juxtaposed with the comfort and laziness? In the next chapter we will focus on this important source of energy, which is TIME. We shall remind ourselves about the value of time and how it must be kept under control. We will expose you to the basic rules of time management in order to effectively maintain and use your energy.

THE GOLDEN NUGGETS

- We must always engage in the process of work and cannot afford to relax because in relaxation, there lies the danger of losing our energy
- You cannot afford to relax because laziness and a high level of comfort, lead to loss of energy
- Comfort is disability, it limits our ability to achieve outstanding success to convert into visible physical world, our ideas and dreams
- The best antidote to feelings of comfort and complacency are crisis and problems
- If you restrain yourself - in food, in pleasure, entertainment - then you gain energy
- If you restrict yourself to something, the energy you have left is reserved, and this reserved energy will be enough to achieve the goals that you set yourself
- Restrictions do not allow us to dissipate energy, but helps us to store it in order to achieve the main thing in life, it helps us not to be distracted by minor things of the moment

SELF-EXAMINATION TEST

It should be noted that only one answer is required for each question or statement. Next to each answer is marked point. The overall score will determine the outcome of your training.

1. Do you think at work, after the end of the working day and the possibility of relaxing?

a. Of course, yes, I do not like to strain. 1 point

b. I think, and quite often, but I cannot afford it, because everything is done in order to live in prosperity and comfort - **2 points**

c. I try not to think about it, because I work for was very good cause, to take care of the family - **3 points**

d. I do not allow myself to think of other things while working as I am fully concentrated on business. For me what is important at that time is the quality of products I produce - **4 points**

2. Comfortable life for me - is:

a. There is enough for everything that I want, to be able to buy everything that is desired. Satisfying my needs - **1 point**

b. Comfort for me - this is what destroys a person. It is not for me an end in itself. The purpose of my life is very important - to help others, and if it requires certain advanced tech equipment, I use them to achieve my goals in life - **4 points**

c. To me and my family it is all about what we dream. New tech products and cozy atmosphere in the hous -. **3 points**

d. To have all the things that I need, but that these are not my immediate goals - **2 points**

3. How will you behave in a situation where you know that comfort and relaxation, is of a negative impact on your work? Will you choose comfort over work?

a. Of course, I'd rather have a rest and enjoy a care-free life. Folk wisdom says, "Work is not a wolf, it's not going to run off to the forest- meaning –the work isn't going anywhere, it can wait." - **1 point**

b. In this situation, I think about how important it is for my physical body at this moment, 'vaca-tion'? If it does not matter, I will not be distracted from the work, I will complete everything with high standard to the end - **4 points**

c. I have thought well about the question, if my relaxed attitude to work will not negatively impact my dream for my family, of course, I will choose the rest and comfort, and then later I can and work - **3 points**

d. I will choose the rest, and then proceed to work. Work is needed in order to climb even higher up the career ladder - **2 points**

4. How much time do you spend daily watching television or surfing the Internet?

a. I can sit for days without getting up, I turned on the TV in my house all day - **0 points**

b. I do not know, but a lot - **1 point**

c. Not more than 2-3 hours - **3 points**

d. I put myself under strict limit by these things - **4 points**

5. Do you think that the restrictions must have a place in your life?

a. No, I value my freedom more than anything, I will not have to put any limit on myself - **0 points**

b. I do not like the idea of the use of violence in relation to myself, life is far too tough to even inconvenience myself - **1 point**

c. Probably, it makes sense, but I have never been able to pull myself together, I constantly break my pledge in regards to self-restraint and cannot fulfill its obligations - **2 points**

d. I keep myself under a "tight rein", I cannot get used to the habit of self-discipline, I am very demanding towards myself, and these habits bring positive changes in my life - **4 points**

TEST RESULTS

From 0 to 7 points - You are a man, accustomed to comfort, any deprivation is perceived by you as a life of tragedy. This is dangerous in that the comfort familiar to you can turn into swamp, which is able to destroy you. You do not really like to work, forgetting that thanks to the process of work you are able to convert energy into a useful product, and as a result of work you have the opportunity for a better place in life.

From 8 to 16 points - You love life, which is filled with comfortable things. But be careful that does not exceed the safety framework and will not leave you in the zone of a lifetime of "disability." You need to learn how to establish a framework in your life, so that you can more effectively accumulate the energy you need to achieve your goals and dreams. To help you in this book try to: examine it carefully and begin to apply the lessons learned on daily basis - the result will be outstanding!

From 16 to 20 points - Congratulations! The scored number of points says that you are not used to a comfortable life. You live a full life, realizing all your talents. You are wise to use self-restraint, which allow you to always accumulate more energy, of which you have directed to your advantage and also for the benefit of others. We wish you success in your way, and do not forget to share his wisdom with his friends and acquaintances, so that their lives become better.

PRACTICAL TASKS

1. Why do you consider comfort and laziness – are the greatest handicap in life? Why do you think a life of pleasure should not become an end in itself for us, and why should we not strive for it? What is the role of restrictions in our lives? List 10 of your inclinations for comfort, and describe how you will deal with them?

2. How do you think you need to use restraint in your life? Write down exactly what and what you want to limit from your life from this moment onward.

CHAPTER 8:

TIME - A MAIN SOURCE OF ENERGY

Time - the limited capital, and if you cannot dispose of them, you cannot manage anything else.

- Peter Drucker (1909-2005), an American scientist of Austrian origin; economist, journalist, educator, one of the most influential theorists of the XX century management

Before we move on to the discussion about the time as the most important source of our energy, let us recall that during the previous chapter, we examined in details about one of the major source of energy, which is self-control. We found out the reason why we should not allow ourselves to relax, because comfort and laziness goes hand in hand? In this chapter we shall be discussing about the value of time and how the ability to control and properly manage your time can help you to uncover the hidden energy.

Time – is life and can be equated to, raw materials and financial resources. No wonder they say: time equals money. I want to tell you, dear reader, that TIME is also an energy source. Our time should be converted into energy, then that energy can be used for product or service, and we don't engage ourselves in vanity, idleness or get affected by lethargy. If every day I will be able to allocate at least 2 hours to ensure that it is invested on serious work and on something worthwhile: to write, to learn, to explore, I can convert the information at my disposal to time energy in creating a useful product, such as a book. And if I just sit back all day long, pointless watching TV, or spend hours chatting on the phone, the time wasted on nonchalant activities cannot be converted into useful energy, denying myself of the profit or value that can be added to my life – wasting time on frivolous activities deplete my life, nothing positive is credited to my value account, no investment no returns. Moreover, I also lose this energy, because valuable thoughts are wasted, they are dispersed somewhere in the clouds, in an insubstantial world of dreams, attention is scattered, there is no concentration. I waste energy and cannot raise it even to do the minimum.

Many people ask me: what is the source of my power? My answer is very simple: **while most people's live are full of activities, I use my time wisely, to pray, talk to God, and to educate myself thereby accumulating the necessary energy for new achievements.**

My life is subordinated to the goal, and strictly regulated because: I have a certain range of activities, which I dedicate myself to. From my schedule I exclude shopping (shopping trips) and going to the cinema, I abandoned idle pastime in the summer on the beach, or other entertainment. My goal - is to save millions of people from hell, and to acquaint them with the living God, who alone can answer all their questions and needs, to bring peace in their hearts. So every day I pray, teach other people, spending time with families and end educating them. I deliberately refuse to waste my time on something that distracts me from my goal, things that defocus my attention and dissipate energy. I consciously direct my resources and energy on something that can bring the most out of the kingdom of God. If you use at least two hours a day to devote to think, to reflect, to read, it would allow you to build and redirect to the proper channel, your direction energy within you, and through this process increasing the volume of your personality. This is where the hidden sources of energy are! But most of us spend our energy on the vanity. Peter Drucker said no wonder that the inability to dispose of such a "limited capital" as time, only shows that we cannot afford to deal with anything else. It therefore makes sense for us to finally realize the value of time and put time in proper perspectives.

THE VALUE OF TIME

Stop acting as if you have 500 years left to live.

- Bill Gates (1955), an American entrepreneur and social activist, philanthropist, one of the founders and former largest shareholder of Microsoft

The value of time cannot be determined. Its real PRICE, it equals OUR LIFE. Time is given to us by God so that we can bear fruit for His kingdom and be able to achieve the things that He has planned for our lives. Do you see the results - results that satisfy God? Means you don't consume recklessly your time on vanity and idleness? If at the end of each day, you do not have a particular result that you can describe in specific numbers, then your time has been captured by vanity. This will have a great impact on your life.

Often we treat time too casually. We treat it as though we have plenty of it, as though we have inexhaustible reserves of time at our disposal. We treat it as if we will always have in the reserve, extra minute, day, month, years or decades .... But it is not so! We treat time carelessly, spending it as we please. Do we realize the value of every moment of our life? That when we spend time, we spend our lives? Did you count how much time you spent on this or that matter? Have you ever thought about how your energy dissipates.

Did you know that if every day you spend 2 hours watching TV, then for 50 years - it will take 14 years of your life, which is given to you only once and will not be able to live it again? If talk over 30 minutes a day on the telephone, it is three and a half years of life. If we add to this 1 hour a day (at most) carried out in the kitchen, it turns out that half of life a person spends on TV, telephone conversations and cooking. Which of these activities will help you reveal your hidden energy? None! These activities will only help in dispelling our energy rather than reserving of adding to our energy reserve. Let's look at the comparison

table of the time spent (assuming 8-hour working day):
During the day, throughout the year within 5 years and 50 years

During the day	During a year	Over 5 years	Over 50 years
10 minutes	7. 5 days	38 days	380 days (1 year)
15 minutes	11 days	57 days	570 days (2 years)
30 minutes	23 days	114 days	1140 days (3. 5 years)
1 hour	46 days (1.5 months)	228 days	2280 days (7 years)
2 hours	91 days (3 months)	456 days (1 year 5)	4563 days (14 years)

On the Internet the following analogy can become applicable, and it will help us to clarify for ourselves the value of time, as a source of stored energy.

Imagine that there is a bank that every morning, credits your account with the amount of $ 86 400. The most interesting thing is that the amount remaining after the daily expenses, cannot "be added to" the expenses of the next day, because your balance is always reset to zero at night . How would you spend the funds in your account? Most likely, you would have made sure to spend every cent of the amount received in the morning. But are you doing so in reality? Probably not, because, in fact, already have such a bank, and the name of the bank –is the 'time' bank.

Every morning, each of us is given a loan of 86 400 seconds, and every night there is not a trace of it left. Time is not transferrable into the future, because every day the bank by the name of "Time" begins with a new countdown. To borrow from the next day is impossible. The way you use the funds allotted to you – is your own business, but you will be liable and be held accountable for each decision you take. You will definitely bear the loss if you did not spend the time currency investment you have been given in a day. [30].

Very imaginative illustration, don't you think so? If we had such a point of view of looking at things, our relationship to time will be different. The following comparisons help us to understand and appreciate the value of time:

In order to understand the price of a year - ask the student remaining in the second year. - To understand the price of a month - ask a mother who gave birth to a premature baby. - To understand the price of one hour - ask the lovers waiting to meet. - To understand the price of one minute - ask a person who missed the train. - To understand the price of a second - just ask someone who escaped the accident. - To understand the price hundredth of a second - just ask the athlete, runner-up [30].

Life is made up of seconds here such minutes, hours, days and years - it is not our property. Life is given to us by God as a rent for a certain period of time, sooner or later we will have to give an account for how we live from day to day; and on what we spend the energy and talents given us by God. Life is given to us only once, so it is necessary to live intentionally, so that the time and energy are not wasted in vain, but that every day of our lives bring benefit and satisfaction to God and humanity. It is important to reflect on life and to remember that it is finite: the years don't go forever, youth will not be repeated, effort and energy spent in vain, will not return, virginity is lost once, and this process is irreversible. It is therefore important to appreciate the life time that you have been given.

We must cherish our time and energy, and therefore should always be aimed at achieving result. After all, the result - this is the equivalent of the time utility lived. We have to manage our time, and it means - to manage our lives. Do not let your time be ruled by circumstances or other people. Plan your time, otherwise people our circumstance will plan it for you. Appreciate your time, by being constantly aware that you have a time frame, a specific period of time available for you to fulfil the purpose of God for your life. The life of each of us is limited in time, so you cannot afford to lose it even for a moment

No wonder Bill Gates exclaimed: *"Stop acting as if you have to live for 500 years!"* - Because you have at your disposal much less time than you can imagine. **If you do not have a specific schedule in life, if you do not plan your time, your life just fly past.** You will not be able to regain the time passed to do what should have been done yesterday, the day before yesterday or a year ago. Analyze your life. How much of your precious time do you spend on the really important things? How busy is the rest of your time?

YOUR TIME SHOULD BE UNDER CONTROL

Time - is the only thing you cannot accumulate, it is not saved and is not increased. It can only be exchanged - for money or knowledge. Time - Is generally the most important.

- **Tadao Yamaguchi,** lecturer, writer, entrepreneur

The main feature is the irrevocability of time - that time cannot be returned, saved, transferred or borrowed.

Therefore, it is very important to learn how to use the resources of time to our maximum benefit. The practice of self-management (or time management) - the art of correct use of time, is becoming increasingly popular. When a person is able to organize his time, job can be done at a lower cost and work schedule are better organized, and as a result of this, better results are obtained. The ability to properly control time can reduce the workload and, as a result, reduce rush and stress. It also reduces the unproductive loss of our energy, that is, mental and physical strength. This should be the aspiration of each one of us!

The freest man is the one who set himself the frame, protecting, above all, his time, so he cannot afford to lose or waste even a moment. Pay attention to the following sentence: MAN, SHAKING OVER EVERY MINUTES OF HIS TIME - THE FREE MAN.

The most important constraints that I need to work out in my life - it's a framework that protects my time.

Enter the restrictions on your time! Why is it vital now try to prove.

The average life expectancy in our country - about seventy years. Simple arithmetic says that the first thing that takes each of our time is- sleep. Therefore, no matter how long a person lived, about a third of his life, will be spent on sleep! Let's count the cost the time spent eating. If we proceed from the assumption that a person takes three meals a day, spending about 20 minutes at one go, in a day the time he spent on meals will be 1 hour. For a month it will not be less than 30 hours, and for the year accumulates to 365hrs, accounting for nearly 15 days! If you multiply 15 days to a year spent on meals, at 50 years of active life, you get 750 days, or 107 weeks, or 25 months. In other words, more than two years of your life is spent for just eating, wow!

In order to free up the time to enhance you doing more important things, than our concern for daily bread, we can try this trick. We should try to shorten the duration of a meal for about 5 minutes. It seems insignificant and trifle, but in terms of days, hours and years of our lives it shows startling figures:

daily - 15 minutes;

month - 460 minutes, or 7.7 hours;

year - 92 hours, or 4 days;

for 50 - 200 days, or more than six months

By reducing food intake by only 5 minutes, we "found" an additional 200 days released or added to our lives! [31]. If this seems low, then consider the following fact: reducing the number of olives in salads, of the first class passengers, exactly one thing, American Airlines has saved the company $ 40 000! [32]. BY SAVING, OR WITH COST-CONSCIOUSNESS ON WASTED TIME, WE ACCUMULATE MUCH-NEEDED ENERGY.

THE BASIC RULES OF TIME MANAGEMENT FOR ENERGY CONSERVATION

It is recommended to make only a certain part of the plan of work (about 60%). You should always leave a certain percentage of the time as a reserve for unexpected visitors, phone calls, emergencies, or the result of underestimation of the length of some cases.

When planning is also recommended

When planning, it is also recommended to use the Pareto Principle or the 20/80 principle, which in general terms is worded as follows: "20% of the effort gives 80% of the results, and the remaining 80% of the effort – gives only 20% of the results." This means that one should not immediately take on the lightest, interesting or requiring a minimum flow of business time. It is necessary to proceed to questions according to their value and importance; **To use your time wisely, which means that the energy and strength, good things should be arranged in order of priority.** To prioritize sufficiently to analyze them based on ABC technique. The essence of this analysis is that by using the letter "A", "B" and "C", all the works are divided into three groups according to their importance (the most important, significant and insignificant (less important)). ABC analysis is based on three laws of:

- Critical tasks account for about 15% of the total number of cases. The contribution of this task to the ultimate objective of about 65%;

- The important tasks account for about 20% of the total number of cases, the significance of which - as about 20%;

- Less important and unimportant tasks account for about 65% of all cases, and their importance is only about 15%.

To use the ABC analysis, you must follow these rules: make a list of tasks;

- organize and prioritize them in order of importance.

- evaluate the tasks in accordance with the categories A, B, C;

- categorize A task to perform;

- delegate the remaining tasks.

An analysis of a list of tasks required to be implemented, can be carried out on the basis of Dwight D. Eisenhower (US President in 1953-1961 GG). Priorities are set according to the criteria such as matter of urgency and importance of the case, therefore, all the cases are divided into 4 groups:

1. immediate (things to do) - they need to perform;

2. term (less important things) - they need to be delegated;

3. less urgent (important tasks) - they are not required to carry out immediately, but can be implemented later.

4. less urgent (less important tasks) - from their implementation, you can refrain [33].

The most important is to keep track of where we get any "leakage" of time. The main "eaters" of our time are:

- TV
- The Internet
- Computer games
- Scandals and clarify the relationship
- Sport events
- Shower
- Endless gatherings with companies
- Queues
- Traffic jams

I invite you, dear reader, to consider
BAD HABITS, STEALING OUR TIME AND METHODS OF COMBATING THEM

1. Mobile phone

It is necessary to control the time taken during phone conversations. If you have the habit of responding to calls at any time of the day, people will control your life, inflicting blows on your energy reserves. If you constantly "hang on the pipe" for hours talking with friends and acquaintances, then you, too, are not to be envied. Highlight special time in your schedule in which you respond to missed calls and systematically make a call, which you really need.

2. Guff

If you live or work among a large number of people, then inevitably you will be tempted to stop to chat for a few minutes, then one, then the other person. However, apart from the loss of time, in the process you waste energy spent for aimless chatting, thus affecting your effectiveness. So short answer, listening to the words of the interlocutor, do not ask a lot of questions. As soon they notice that you aren't paying attention to their conversation, they stop talking. Do not let the other person diverge away from the essence of the conversation and talk about everything. After welcoming person, then go to work, learn to express your thoughts briefly. Also, you can help with headphones: go to them, even if you do not listen to anything. This will help you not to be distracted and at the same time, prevent others from distracting you.

3. Checking the mail

E-mail - a very important tool for organizing your life. Many questions can and should be dealt with by e-mail, as written thought is always more complete and capacious. When a man says he is thinking about how to better articulate his thoughts, and to whom it is addressed, the issue is much easier and faster to understand and to take measures to resolve it. Thus, e-mail serves as a stop for a certain setting goals and descriptions of events. The interviewee has to communicated specifically, cutting off all unnecessary.

However, when working with e-mails, it is also important to be careful. You must accustom yourself to check your mail on a schedule. By doing so unchecked, you can easily break your plans that will lead to the loss of not only time but also energy. To do this, turn off on the incoming e-mail alerts, and choose for yourself the email scan mode in at least about 2 times a day, for example, at 12.00 and 16.00.

Know how to skillfully manage your time, take good care of every minute, gain more time, and learn to accumulate the necessary energy available to you. To achieve this, we cannot do without the imposition of the specific scopes and limitations. As said Meg Whitman (1956), an American manager from 1998 to 2008 headed the company eBay, runs Hewlett-Packard Corporation in 2011:

"If you give any team an unlimited time or resources to carry out a task, it rarely brings the desired results ... Limitations force us to concentrate." The great strength lies in the self-limitation: without it is impossible TO DISCOVER OUR STORED ENERGY SOURCE.

So, in this chapter, we have considered such an important source of energy, that is TIME. Through our studies we are able see a new way to discover the value of time and learned about how the ability to control, and properly manage your time, can help us to uncover our hidden energy. In the next chapter we will study one important source of energy - discipline. We'll talk about why discipline - is the key to success, as well as a detailed look at the components of discipline: perseverance, persistence and organization, without which the discipline is unattainable.

THE GOLDEN NUGGETS

- Time - this is also ENERGY
- Our time should be converted into energy, then that energy can be used for products or services, and we don't engage ourselves vanity, idleness or be affected with lethargy
- The main feature of the time is that, it is irrevocable - that time cannot be returned, saved, transferred, or borrowed
- A man shaking over every minute of his time - the freest man
- The most important constraints that I need to work out in my life - is the framework that protects my time
- To use your time wisely, means that the energy and strength, good things should be arranged in order of priority
- The level of human respect to themselves is determined by how they can follow and established their plans
- If you do not have a specific schedule in life, if you do not plan your time, your life just fly past
- The value of time cannot be determined. Its real PRICE, equals OUR LIFE
- We need to take care of our time and energy, and therefore should always be aimed at the result

SELF-EXAMINATION TEST

Rate yourself on a scale: 0 - 1 almost never - sometimes 2 - 3 often - almost always

1. I reserve at the beginning of the working day time for preparatory work, planning.	
2. I delegate everything I can reassign	
3. I write down fixed goals and objectives, with a timetable for their implementation	
4. For each official document, I process them on time and finally	
5. Every day, I make a list of upcoming cases, ordered by priority. The most important things I do in the first place	
6. I release my time from prying phone calls, unscheduled meetings, unexpected meetings	
7. Every day, I apportion the workload in accordance with my performance schedule	
8. In my daily plans I always allow a window, allowing me to respond to the current problems	
9. I will extend my activities in such a way that first of all concentrate on the few "vital" problems	
10. I know how to say "no" when my time compromised by others, and I need to do more important things	
VERDICT:	

TEST RESULTS

From 0-15 points - Unfortunately, you do not plan your time, and you are at the mercy of external circumstances. You lose too much energy, not knowing how to properly handle the issue of time. But to achieve your goals and succeed more than you are now, you need to make a list of priorities and stick to it. You will succeed.

From 16-20 points - You are trying to take control of your time, but do not always achieve this success. In your life, there are many factors that take you away, depriving not only the time, but the effort and energy. You need to become more consistent in maintaining the framework of your time, to be a success.

From 21-25 points - Not bad, you have a fairly high level of self-management, that is, the ability to manage your time resources. This allows you to store energy, and you do not expend it in vain. Continue to work hard to "fuss over every minute of your time," it will help you more successful in life.

From 26-30 points - Congratulations, you can serve as a model for anyone who wants to learn how to efficiently use his time! In this regard, you have enough strength and energy for any cause for which ever you have decided to take. This valuable skills, do not forget to share with people around you.

PRACTICAL TASKS

1. Describe why you often waste time. Choose at least five points.
2. Develop a plan, describe the specific steps, you are going to take to keep time under control?

CHAPTER 9:

DISCIPLINE - A MAIN SOURCE OF ENERGY

Our study on how TO DISCOVER YOUR SOURCE OF LATENT ENERGY, continues. This book is about ENERGY." reminding ourselves that according to the law of conservation of energy, the total energy of an isolated system remains constant- it is said to be conserved over time. Energy can neither be created nor destroyed: rather, it is transformed from one form to another. In the previous chapter we explored, TIME such an important source of energy. In this chapter, we are waiting for the study of a very important energy source called discipline. We find out why discipline is the key to success, as well as look at the components of discipline: perseverance, persistence and organization., without which discipline is unattainable.

In 1960, the group "The Beatles" was still an obscure school rock band. In Germany, during their time in Hamburg they found the owner of the cavern, who had the habit of inviting a variety of rock bands to attract the attention of the public loitering. The scheme was fairly simple: musicians performed for long sessions without any pauses. While the crowds were moving back and forth, the music had to keep on playing. But this is not that promising, Hamburg musician do not have the patience to continue, also due to the fact that the owner of the club was not willing to pay much for their show, the acoustics were bad, and the audience is not the most enterprising and rewarding. How could this initiate a dizzying success of the Fab Four? But the secret was still.

Let's take a closer look at what musician do in "tours" of such. In the best case, it was necessary to perform for a maximum of one hour, during which the musicians played only hits, and which is repeated at every performance. In Hamburg, the picture was very different: they had to play for at least eight hours in a row! It was in this scenario that the "Beatles" concerts came to Hamburg for a one and a half years - between 1960 to 1962 – for five times. In the first visit, they gave 106 concerts, the length of five or more hours a night, second visit - 92 concert, the third - 48, conducted on stage, a total of 172 hours. The last two soon added to their practice further 90 hours. Thus, in a relatively short period of time the novice musicians managed to play for 270 nights.

Here is what John Lennon said about that period of time: "We have got better and gain confidence. Otherwise, it could not be, because we had to play every evening and night. The fact that they were foreigners, had to be very helpful. To reach them, we had to try our best, to invest our heart and soul in music. In Liverpool, we were in the best case for one hour, and we play only hits, the same in every presentation. In Hamburg, we had to play for eight hours in a row, so whether we want it, or not, we have to try to do our best "[11].

By the time "The Beatles" was ripe for the first big hit, they had given about 1,200 live concerts (!) - An incredible amount for most beginners' advanced groups. Many teams do not have time to "give" such number of times of performance, even for all the time of their existence. It turns out, that allowed "The Beatles" forge ahead and become the best - it is their "hard labor" in Hamburg. Those countless concerts became their school, so that they were able to succeed!

Historian Philip Norman Group states: "They left nothing that is not presenting, and returned in fine form. They learned not only stamina. They had to learn a great number of songs - cover version of all the works, which exist only rock 'n' roll and even jazz. Until Hamburg they did not know what discipline is on the scene. But when they returned, they played in a style not unlike any other. It was the discovery of their own ". [11]

DISCIPLINE - is key to success. So what happened to an unknown group of musicians who have found the strength to discipline themselves to play in countless concerts. Discipline had become for them, a source of energy from which they drew strength for their dizzying success. One of the important properties of the discipline is consistency. Which was demonstrated by the band "The Beatles". They consistently performed from one concert to another, and that led them to succeed. You could say that fate itself had brought them to the stage of the Hamburg club. If they did not go through this "hard school", who knows, we would not have ever heard the names of illustrious members of the Fab Four?

What is it - "discipline"? Let's open the dictionary and read. Discipline (from the Latin disciplina- regulation of life, training, instruction, system, military rule, it is derived from the Latin discipulus- student.) - The rules of conduct of the person corresponding to the norms accepted in the society and the requirements of the rules of regulations (https://ru.wikipedia.org). Also, under the discipline of the organization and involve decency. **Disciplined people - is collected and organized person who knows how to keep everything in order.**

Disciplined people - are those that:

- are always "here and now"
- healthy emotionally and physically
- persons who understand situations and circumstances
- they always achieve the desired result

DISCIPLINE - A KEY TO SUCCESS

Is success by happenstance? Or is achievement by coincidence? No, each of them requires hard work, coupled with discipline. **The man who disciplines himself, always has the best results and the best performance.** For example, great people are diligent in all things. They are so zealous that they do not put off until tomorrow what you can do today. Diligence is to do everything you need to do at once - NOW. Do not put off until tomorrow what you can do today, there is what it takes to be highly organized.

When a person does not delay in the case he handles, and is consistent at all times, he manages more than the average people around him, he is able to release more time for new tasks, this improves the quality of executed works, produced by self-organization skills. This enhances our reputation in the eyes of other people and thereby putting us more on the competitive edge.

"Good artists copy, great artists steal, but real artists - perform the order on time", - said Steve Jobs (1966-2011), an American entrepreneur, widely regarded as a pioneer in the era of IT-technologies, co-founder, chairman and Corporation CEO Apple. It is therefore important to do everything at once, without delaying matters indefinitely.

SUCCESSFUL PEOPLE NEVER PUT OFF FOR TOMORROW WHAT THEY CAN DO TODAY. They seek to ensure that the distance between the desire (or solution) to do something and implementation process is reduced to a minimal. Efficiency, which leads to success - is when a person is making every effort to ensure that every of his decision is sound and lead to a result. In other words, the ability to minimize the distance between the decision and the action to be effective. You can output the following formula:

SOLUTION + action = RESULT/EFFICIENCY

If you live by this principle, then, of course, in life you will succeed. This should be your way of life. Make the decision to develop the habits of Highly Effective People:

1. Learn to discipline yourself

2. Make a decision not to delay your case in the "back burner" - to do everything in the first 72 hours

3. You must develop the habit of starting to do something within the first 72 hours (3 days) after the decision. It is better to have a supply of spare time to the end of the deadline, make it a habit to perform the task standing before you, so that you avoid doing the work in hurry. The first 72 hours - that's the best time to perform tasks,

implement ideas and decisions. People who do not lay their cases indefinitely, but perform them within the first 72 hours always:

- achieve the highest results
- are the most effective
- included in the 3% most influential people in the world

It is particularly important to embody the ideas and carry out tasks for 72 hours because you cannot predict your life for more than 3 days, you do not know what might happen next. In life, too, in is a very important habit to act instantly. What does this mean? Decide for 5 seconds does not mean to act immediately. In the first five seconds after you find important information for yourself, take enough decision for how long you intend to execute it.

This principle does not mean that we need to break away and flee in a hurry to make schedules. It states that the need to quickly start not only in the implementation of the action, but also in the work of the internal preparatory work on yourself, which apparently it cannot be seen. *"When I decide to do something, then I do it quickly"*, Carlos Slim (1940), a Mexican businessman of Arab origin, the son of immigrants Maronite from Lebanon, a billionaire, one of the richest people in the world, according to "Forbes", in 2010, 2011 2012 and 2013 was the richest man in the world. NEED TO TEACH YOURSELF TO MAKE DECISIONS AND LAUNCH PROCESSES TO IMPLEMENT THEM WITHIN 5 SECONDS

Let your life will become a credo:
- to bring the follow through
- keep your promises

PERSEVERANCE - A NECESSARY QUALITY OF DISCIPLINE

If you really want something, you have to achieve this on your own and with all determination. Nobody is going to give you this, and if you hesitate or doubt, you will surely fail.

- Chuck Norris

Persistence allows us to store energy. People who know how to be assertive can be unflappable, unwavering, that under any circumstances, no matter what happens, they do not give up, but continue to move forward, always full of energy. Success comes the way of such people. These people are assertive in their studies, and therefore receive a red diploma, showing persistence in search of work, and as a result of this wonderful quality, they find better jobs. They show perseverance in everything, whatever they are doing so that fate can smiles at them. In the end, it is this quality allows people to achieve greatness.

Even when the situation is very serious, do not turn off the chosen path, be faithful to your purpose. Very easy to quit and give up when there comes a day when we feel that we are at an impasse, and everything is not so, as we currently have planned and imagined. *"Discouragement and failure are two of the most faithful steps to* *success"* - Dale Carnegie argued. Great quote at all times! When you feel depressed and lack motivation, you know that you're nearly there. Winston Churchill (1874-1965), British statesman and politician, Prime Minister of the United Kingdom, owned by great words: *"Never, never, never give up!"* At intransigence just keep going and doing, even through the "cannot" to what you Must do.

The student came to the Master and began to complain of her hard life. And asked the Master for advice what to do when something challenging happens, and then came over to the master with a heavy heart. The teacher silently got up, set a four-pot with water. In one, he put a wooden chock, in the other - a carrot, the third - an egg, and in the fourth - the crushed coffee beans. After a while he brought them out of the bowls.

- What changed? - asked the teacher.

- Nothing. - The student replied.

The teacher nodded, and put all the pots on the fire. When the water was boiling, he again put back wooden chock in pot, in the other - a carrot, the third - the egg, and in the fourth - coffee.

- What changed? - The teacher asked again.

- All that is expected to happen. Carrot and the egg were cooked, a piece of wood did not change, and the coffee beans were dissolved in boiling water, - said pupil.

- This is a superficial view of things, - answered the Teacher. - Look closely. Carrot seethed in water and from being hard to becoming soft, easily break-able. Even outwardly it began to look different. The wood did not change. Egg did not change the appear-

ance, but has become a solid mass, it has changed from the fragile substance that is easily breakable to a solid mass. Coffee colored the water, giving it a new taste and flavor. Water - is our life, and the fire — equals our challenges and adverse circumstances. Carrot, tree, eggs and coffee - are types of people. They are all in difficult moments of life changing in many ways.

Man as 'carrots'. These are - the majority. These people just in everyday life seem to be solid, and in the moments of life troubles become soft and slippery. Such "carrot", as a rule, easily become victims of the prevailing circumstances, they want to have it all, like many people. They made their fortunes, sometimes are also, successful merchants, politicians and prognosticators.

Man as 'tree'. Such are small. These people do not change, they remain themselves in all situations. They tend to be unmoved, internally calm and solid. Such people show us that any difficult life circumstances — is just the life that always comes white behind the black stripe.

Human as 'egg'. It is those who that life's adversities tend to make them stronger. Such people are very, very small. In ordinary life, they are imperceptible, but in times of sudden "hardship" and they harden up to overcome the external circumstances.

- And what about the coffee? - The student said.

- Oh, that's the fun part!

The Man 'coffee'. Coffee beans are exposed to adverse circumstances of life disappeared in the environment, turning ordinary water into delicious, aromatic drink! There are special people. They are in unit. They did not so much change. The influence of trouble had transformed them, circumstances of life, turned them into something beautiful, they become benefiting from every situation and changing for the better, the lives of all the people around them.

So said the Master, happy sipping aromatic coffee cup.

We all need to become "men-coffee": those who transform, change adversity into positive effects in life. These people have the strength not just to accumulate, store energy, but also to redirect it in a positive way, no matter how the situation unfolded. This is the most valuable asset that you can have with you. DIFFICULTIES Puts target significance for us, AND ONLY ALLOW DISCIPLINE OVERCOME THEM.

CONSISTENCY - A NECESSARY QUALITY OF DISCIPLINE

It was character that got us out of bed, commitment that moved us into action, and discipline that enabled us to follow through..

- Zig Ziglar (1926 p.),
Writer, lecturer

Discipline is always associated with persistence - the ability to bring any matter to an end. A disciplined person is committed to ensuring that he follows through, no matter the level of effort from him as it may be required. Where efforts have been made, there is no room for laziness. As you know, one only realizes until the end of the idea a lot better than the 100 who started and abandoned. Abandoned projects remind me of a man who every hour puts on the kettle to drink tea. He pours water, tea leaves and fell asleep. To boil the kettle, you need about10 minutes. To make a cup of tea you need tea leaves and sugar. After 8 minutes, he recalls that the sugar is not in the tea, and he then turns off the kettle. It was not boiled. He goes for the sugar. It is now getting to about an hour, and again puts the kettle. At least this should boil for 10 minutes. But after 8 minutes the phone rang. He again turns off the kettle and began to talk with a friend for more than 30 minutes, he says, he wanted a cup of tea. But there is no time, and also the desire to have tea had disappeared.

Spent time: 2 x 8 minutes, when the tea is almost boiled. And hour to hike for sugar. What was the result? NOTHING.

Those who begin it from start to the end, certainly will have the chance to take advantage of opportunities.

To do this:

- Learn how to move without stopping

- persevere

- Find the best knowledge to move quickly and correctly.

- IF YOU GO ON CONTINUOUSLY with your goals, you attract that ENERGY that is needed to accomplish them.

It is important to be in constant movement forward, it gives us energy and strength. This is the main key to success. *"Sage is constant as the sun. Fool changeable as the moon"*, - said Seneca, the Roman Stoic philosopher, poet and statesman, Nero's tutor and one of the leading representatives of Stoicism.

A disciplined person brings to the end of every decision, even if no one knows about it. This means that human decency, primarily determined by the ability not to break the data of promises to himself. Agree, this is at odds with our notions of decency: sometimes we are more concerned about how to be perfect in the eyes of others, but on the promises made to ourselves, you easily close your eyes, imagine forgiving the failure to comply. But the situation is exactly the opposite! Your life will not reach its maximum, if you do not learn in the first place, in good faith to fulfill the promises made to yourself, even if no one knows about it.

You have to be very organized person to take up the case on your own, without an influence from above. Statistics show that most people start to do something, when someone from the outside poses some tough timeframe or conditions. However, what people do under the pressure from the outside, does not remain with him for a long time.

FOR, IN LIFE, MAN KEEPS only what he does through his own decisions. Perhaps this is why initiative - is a property, which so eagerly gets the managers in all companies. Do not miss the initiative. When you come to a good idea, start implementing it without orders from above. When the surrounding sees how serious you are about the case, you will be noted. No one controls those who sit at the top. If you want to join them, begin to exercise self-discipline in your actions.

BEING ORGANIZED - THE MOST IMPORTANT QUALITY OF DISCIPLINE

In order to organize your life, you must be disciplined. Do people have a disciplined schedule for their lives? Lack of organization and order prevents a person to change, and such a person to properly align priorities and values. Undisciplined person is too lazy to take the time to organize his life. He does not manage to solve the main problem, but rather runs from one matter to the other urgent matters. And so life goes, never reaching the implementation of major life goal or dream.

You have only 24 hours in a day, so the time should be organized so that you can reach a maximum daily benefit in the implementation of your global purpose in life. Perhaps today you have failed to address important issues in your life because you have gone through a lot of serious problems and challenges. People who find themselves in a dead-end, I recommend that they organize their life! In our lives there are plenty of obstacles to becoming more organized and in striving to achieve our goals, and one of them is laziness. And no one, except us, is unable to cope with it. It is our responsibility: either remain at the same level, or roll down or pull ourselves together, to organize and discipline ourselves to live the life we want to live, not the one we are forced to. **When a man disciplines himself, he opens an internal energy source, he accumulates it and releases it.**

DISCIPLINE, EQUALS LABOR, TIME AND SELF-RESTRAINT - THIS IS ONE OF THE MOST POWERFUL WAY TO CONVERT ENERGY. So, in this chapter the subject of our study of the source of energy, -DISCIPLINE. In the next and final chapter, we will look at how to continue to share power with others, and thus to stay alive? We will discuss the factors that allow a person to renew energy, as well as those that lead to a loss of human energies.

THE GOLDEN NUGGETS

- Discipline - is the key to success
- Disciplined people - are collected and organized, who knows how to keep everything in order
- The man who disciplines himself, always has the best results and the best performance
- Perseverance allows us to store energy
- Even when the situation is very serious, do not turn away from the chosen path, be loyal to your goal
- If we have difficulties in making the goal more important for us, only discipline allows us to overcome them
- Discipline is always associated with persistence
- If you continuously stick to the set goals, you attract the necessary energy
- A disciplined person brings to the end of every decision, even if no one knows about it
- To organize your life, you must be disciplined
- When a man disciplines himself, he opens an internal energy source, he accumulates it and releases it
- Discipline, as well as labor, time and self-restraint – is one of the most powerful methods of energy conversion

SELF-EXAMINATION TEST

In each of the 13 questions select only one answer.
Questions:

1. Do you have goals in life, to which you aspire?

a. Yes;

b. Is it possible to have some kind of purpose, since life is so changeable?;

c. I have a main goal, and I submit my life to achieve them;

d. Goal I have, but my work does little for me to achieve them.

2. Do you make plans for the week using the Weekly, or special notes, etc.?

a. Yes;

b. There are no plans;

c. I cannot say yes or no, because I keep in mind the main proceedings, and the current day plan - in my head or on a piece of paper;

d. I tried to make a plan, using the weekly, but then I realized that it does nothing;

3. "Chastise" Do you report yourself for failure in your scheduled duty for the week, for the day?

a. "To report" in those cases when I see the fault, laziness or clumsiness;

b. "To report", in spite of any subjective or objective reasons;

c. Now and everything is blamed each other, why "chastise" myself;

d. Adhere to this principle: what has been done today - is good, but it was not the best possible - performance, maybe some other time.

4. How do you conduct your notebook with business phones numbers, acquaintances, relatives?

a. I am the master (mistress) of my notebook. I record the names the way I like. If I need a phone number, then I will find it;

b. I change my note containing my phone records quite often. Because they get "muddled up". When rewriting the phone number I try to do everything "properly", however, the more I use the note the more I put in arbitrary entries;

c. I enter the all phone numbers, of my family member, business and acquaintances with my proper handwriting, I don't bother myself with the sequence of the arrangement of the entries.

d. Using the conventional system, in accordance with the alphabet, I write down the name, phone number and, if necessary, and additional information.

5. You are surrounded by things you frequently use. What are the principles guiding the arrangement of those things?

a. Everything is, anywhere;

b. Adhere to the principle: everything – in its own place;

c. Periodically put the things in group arrangement of things and objects. Then I put them where necessary. After some time again put them in groups;

d. I consider that this question has nothing to do with self-organization.

6. Can you say at the end of the day, where, how much and for what reasons you had to waste time in vain?

a. I can say about the lost time;

b. I can only say about the place where it was lost in vain;

c. If the time lost was paid in money, then I would have believed it;

d. Is not only a good idea where, how and why time was lost, but I also to seek methods of reducing losses in the same situations.

7. How do you act when the meeting (the meeting) starts pouring out of the "sieve"

a. I propose to draw attention to the subject matter;

b. At any meeting or assembly and there always something right and something empty. The alternation of the two takes place a meeting. And there is nothing you can do about it - you have to listen;

c. Plunge into "oblivion";

d. Start to deal with those things as they come.

8. You have to make a presentation. Do you attach importance not only to the content of the report, but also its duration?

a. I pay close attention to the content of the report.

b. I think that the duration must be determined only approximately.

c. If the report is interesting, then time should be given to finish it;

d. Spend equal attention to the content and the pro-expectancy of the report, as well as its variants, depending on the time.

9. Do you try to use every minute to accomplish the conceived?

a. I try, but It does not always work for personal reasons (lack of energy, bad mood, etc.);

b. I do not aspire to it, because I believe that we should not be small-minded in terms of time;

c. Why strive for it, if the time is still not overtaking;

d. I try, no matter what.

10. What task instructions fixation system do you use?

a. I write put down the tasks in weekly terms and when the tasks is to be performed;

b. I put down the most important task in weekly term and perform them. The "Trifle" task I try to remember. If you forget about the "little things" I do not consider it a disadvantage;

c. I try to remember assignments, tasks and

requests, as it trains memory. However, I must admit that the memory often fails me;

d. Adhere to the principle of "reverse memory"; it lets me remember the assignments and tasks and he who gives them. If this is important, for I will not forget and it calls for my immediate execution.

11. Similarly, whenever you come for business meetings, and you are the coordinator of the meeting?

a. I come earlier for at least 5-7 minutes before the meeting;

b. I come just in time to the begin the event;

c. As a general rule, late;

d. Always late, but I try to arrive early or on time;

e. I need help to learn how to not be late.

12. What value do you attach to the timeliness of assignments, requests, orders?

a. I consider that the timely performance - one of the most important indicators of the ability to work. But sometimes I fail in this area.

b. I'm part of the case that is not always able to finish my assignment in the allotted time;

c. In a timely manner to accomplish anything - this is the right chance to get a new job or assign-ment. Diligence always is punished, therefore I do a little to retain my job;

d. I prefer less talk about timeliness, and to perform tasks and assignments on time.

13. **You have promised to do something or do something to help someone else. But circumstances have changed in a way that is difficult to fulfill the promise. How are you going to behave?**

a. Inform of change in circumstances and the impossibility to fulfill the promise;

b. I try to say that circumstances have changed and it is difficult to fulfill the promise, but at the same time to say that we should not lose hope in the fulfillment of the promises;

c. I will try to fulfill the promise. If am able - well, if not, I will explain the reasons for non-compliance;

d. I don't always give promise to man, but if we promise, I will fulfill the promise, come what may.

TEST RESULTS

Keyed get quantitative estimates of the selected answer choices. Next, add up all the assessment and the resulting amount as correlated with the results of the evaluation, given that after the key to the test.

Ans	Points												
wers	Question number												
	1	2	3	4	5	6	7	8	9	10	11	12	13
a	4	6	4	0	0	2	3	2	3	6	6	3	2
b	0	0	6	0	6	1	0	6	0	1	6	0	0
c	6	3	0	0	0	0	0	-	0	1	0	6	0
d	2	0	0	6	0	6	6	-	6	0	0	-	6
e	-	0	-	-	-	-	-	-	-	-	0	-	-

Less than 63 points. We are sorry, but discipline is not inherent in you. It is necessary to analyze your actions, what you spend your time to find out what can help you become more efficient. To become a disciplined person you need will and perseverance.

From 63-71 points. Not bad, discipline inherent in you, however, it needs to be even in greater development. Do not stop there. Organization brings the greatest effect to those who continue to cultivate this quality, necessary for full disclosure of the hidden energy in each of us.

From 72-78 points. Congratulations, you are a disciplined person! Your ability to organize things and stick to the schedule can only be envied. You actually do not allow leakage of the energy associated with the lack of organization.

PRACTICAL TASKS

1. What did you learn from the history of the formation of the group "The Beatles"? How can you apply to your life, the principles that have helped them achieve a resounding success?

2. What is discipline? What is peculiar to a disciplined person? How does discipline help to reveal a hidden sources of energy?

CHAPTER 10:

HOW TO SHARE ENERGY WITH OTHERS AND STAY ALIVE?

So, the book, which deals with HOW TO DISVOVER YOUR SOURCE OF LATENT ENERGY is coming to an end. We are with you, dear reader, at the final tail end of the final pages of this study. Throughout the book, we constantly repeat to you the law of conservation of energy, that, the total energy of an isolated system remains constant- it is said to be conserved over time. Energy can neither be created nor destroyed: rather, it is transformed from one form to another, which means that energy is always available. In the previous chapter, the subject of our research was crucial energy source called discipline. In this chapter, we will focus on how to continue to share power with others and at the same time stay alive. We shall talk about the factors that allow a person to renew energy, as well as those that lead to a loss of human energies. Well, let's start ...

In our daily lives we often give ourselves, our strength and vitality to others in order that they may recover to feel much better, sharing with them in their sorrows, pains and worries. Sometimes we do not realize that what we do, the impact of this is very heavy on our lives because of the load we carry, and we ourselves do not control these processes. Often we are involved in situations, as the appliance. The result is that the energy that the people enjoy from us they take it without our consent. On this we will look at this story;

A PARABLE OF A DONOR

He sat down beside me in the queue to the therapist. The queue stretched slowly in a slightly dark corridor, it was impossible to read. I was pleased as he approached me.

- *How long have you been waiting? He asked.*
- *For a while, I replied. – I have been waiting for over two hours.*
- *Shouldn't it be on a ticket system, first come first serve bases?*
- *Yes it is but - sadly people are ignoring the process, they come in and push in line - everyone is trying to get through to see the therapist without following the process.*
- *You should not let them through if they came after you. - He suggested.*
- *I don't have the strength to fight with them - I admitted. It was difficult for me to make it here in the first place.*

He looked at me and asked cautiously:
- *Are you a donor?*
- *Why should I be a "donor"? - I replied abruptly - No, no I'm not a donor ...*
- *Yes you are! I can see ...*
- *Oh, No! I donated my blood once and never again – I fainted the first time, the first and last time.*

- *And how often do you faint?*
- *Well, it happens, I often fall when I walk and fall asleep during the day.*
- *This is should not be the case. It seems you have very low energy level. Your energy vessel is empty.*
- *Which vessel?*
- *The energy vessel, - he explained patiently.*

Now I looked at him. He was cute, but a little strange. Young, not more than thirty years old, but his eyes! These were the eyes of the wise turtle Tortilla, from the tale I was told as a child. His eyes had so much light, and they had so much under-standing and sympathy that I just fell into a stupor.

- *Do you get sick often? - He asked.*
- *No, why? I rarely get sick. I'm actually very strong. You should not think that I am weak just because I am tiny*
- *But your constitution still can say something to me. And what about your relationships with parents?*
- *They are not very good - I admitted. – I almost do not remember my father, he left us when we were little children. And with my mother.. oh it is difficult! I am still a baby in her eyes and she keeps demanding of me what I am not, she is trying to get me to live her life by her own rules*
- *So what do you do?*
- *I oppose when I have energy. And when I don't, I cry.*
- *Does it help?*

- *Well, a little bit. Until the next quarrel. Once or twice a week. Well, sometimes three.*
- *Have you tried not fueling the fire?*
- *What fire? I don't understand?*
- *Look. You Mom provoke you to react? You respond, by giving her exactly what she wants. Your mum knows the button to press. Like electric she switch you on. Then she starts to feed off your energy and when your energy is zapped, she is fine, and you feel bad. Am I right?*
- *Yes you are! Tell me more, how can I put a stop to this?*
- *So stop turning on - he advised. – There is no other way.*
- *But how, if she knows all my weaknesses and uses them against me? - I get agitated. - She knows me inside out!*
- *Exactly, those weaknesses are like buttons. She pressed the button and you turned on. So when she touches those points there are a connection and the leak of energy takes place! Just as it had being taught in the school of physics.*
- *Yes, I remember something like that was taught ...*
- *And the laws of physics, by the way, are common to all including humans. In the School of Life, we are often given poor marks.*
- *What do you mean by school of life?*
- *Life in itself is a school and we often fail in life because we neglect to heed to her lessons.*
- *Oh, it is so true, my lack of attention to the school of life, have caused me a lot of pain.*

- *While the lesson is not learned – it will certainly be repeated. Life is a good teacher; it demands 100% performance from its pupils!*
- *I have no strength to pay due attention to life's lessons. You see, even this visit to the doctor was a struggle. I can barely move my feet.*
- *So how often do you have health issues?*
- *Only this week, and I don't know what happened. I just don't feel well, like I don't have the strength to do anything?*
- *Do you mind sharing with me how your week was?*
- *Ok, it was a regular week, as always, work, and home the same routines. Oh and arguments with mum a couple of times, of course. And there was one insignificant situation with my co-worker. Nothing serious, just a misunderstanding. I spent some hours on the phone trying to help one of my friends to resolve a problem. But at the end I felt as if I had plowed on all week!*
- *Well, maybe, you plowed, but you did not notice. What were you resolving on the phone?*
- *Oh, yes it is garbage. My girlfriend problems, she had to speak out. I was just a shoulder for her to cry on.*
- *Your shoulder?*
- *I mean, I had to listen to her! Comfort and support her, give her smart advises. And thought that I should not complain to her about my problems because she has enough of her own.*
- *I think you should not have offered her your 'shoulder'. She loaded you with all her negative*

baggage and you responded to her with a positive energy in the form of advice and support. Yes it was a seemingly nice deed, you were a good friend but you were not good to yourself, you did not recharge your own energy.

    -    *I had to, that is what friends do. We support each other.*

    -    *That's it, "each other." And you get the friend-ship "one-sided". You supported her, but who support you?.*

    -    *I do not know ... well I cannot turn a blind eye, if a friend needs my help then I will do all I can to help.*

    -    *Are you friends? Or she is just using you? Why don't you test her? Start a conversation with her and tell her about your problems and see what happens. You might wonder how this will help save your energy.*

    -    *Yeah, you know, it would be nice ... to have more energy. Now when you have told me this I see that it is accurate. After I talk to her I feel like I unloaded the cargo.*

    -    *But let me ask you. Do you have your own problems?*

    -    *Yes, plenty. For example, my ex-husband. I love him as a person. And maybe a little bit more. But he already has another family and it is not going well. I think she charmed him with magic. I feel sorry for him because he's a good man! Still, he is the down to earth man ...*

    -    *Do you enjoy these experiences?*

- *What do you mean, how can I enjoy someone else's misery? After talking to him I am thinking of how can I help him and I just cannot find solution..*
- *And how old is your ex-husband?*
- *He's a little older than me. But does it matter?*
- *It is important. Adult man himself should be in a position to solve his own problems. If he wants to, of course. And if not he is accustomed to shifting them to others. Do you communicate with him often?*
- *Yes of course! He comes to visit our children. This is when he shares these problems with his wife with me.*
- *And you feel pity for him?*
- *Well, of course, I empathize with him. He is just so bad ...*
- *And you, therefore, are feeling very good?*
- *No, I also feel bad.*
- *Just think about it. How are you able to assist him? Do you just want to add his "bad" to your "bad"?*
- *No! No! I give him what he does not have in his family. Understanding... support ... Heat ...*
- *And in return?*
- *I do not know. Gratefulness, perhaps?*
- *Well yes. He is grateful for what you give him and he takes it to his family, because they demand this, and he does not have it himself. He takes it from you. So, do you know why you're exhausted?*
- *No, I was just about to find it out from the therapist. - she said.*

- *The therapist treats the symptoms. Well, prescribes vitamins, assign you to go to get massages. And yet! And the problems persist.*
- *What are the causes?*
- *You do not love yourself. You are trying to love others without loving yourself first. And it's so energy consuming! And you feel chattered.*
- *So what should I do?*
- *I would advise you to look to yourself, look at yourself in the mirror and talk to yourself. Then think, do you really need to stretch yourself as you are doing, so that others can feel better at your expense? Zapping your life energy? Take them all off your shoulders! Stop being a donor. At least temporarily! And start loving yourself, pamper yourself, feed yourself. Then after a while you will be filled up with energy and shine just like the light in the dark! And your eyes will light up with high energy. You'll see!*

He spoke enthusiastically, his eyes were burning, and I thought - what an interesting person! Such a clever man! I wonder what he does for a living.

- *Well, you taught me to live, and you, yourself is sick too! - I suddenly realized.*
- *No, I'm not sick. I'm an electrician. I just had a lunch break. By the way, the break is ended. There is my partner with a ladder, am now going to change the light bulb! Goodbye and good health to you! Mental - first and foremost and enough of being a donor!*

So I sat there with my mouth wide open, watching as my acquaintance jumped up and joined the older man, who really went down the hall with a ladder. My God, I just did not notice that he was wearing a blue jumpsuit, a uniform? Probably because of his eyes – I could not stop looking in his eyes.

And I felt strange warmth in my chest, as if something is poured there, a pleasant and refreshing feeling. I even felt that my energy is coming back to me. "The laws of physics, by the way, are common to all as he said. Suddenly I clearly remembered the lesson of physics that about energy and its flow. When water is poured from one level to another, it will rise. And vice versa. Perhaps while we were talking, he has transferred his high positive energy unto me.

I jumped up and ran down the corridor, to catch up with him.

-    Wait a minute! This is what happens? You too a donor?

-    Donor – he smiled. – But I, unlike you, I share power voluntarily, because I have it in abundance!

-    Why is it you have many? What is your secret?

-    It is very simple. Never allow yourself to be drain by others, be in control of your life and your responses to others. That's it!

He turned to his partner in the office – to fix the light.

I thoughtfully went back down the hall, and then back to the waiting room; I still want to be a donor but now I know I must first pour Love to my life-blood, filled it the brim and then I will be sure to learn to give light as I will have it in abundance –

just like the handsome electrician with wise eyes of turtle Tortilla.

We just need to learn to share our energy not to our detriment, so that one day we will not find ourselves with nothing for our life. If you want to become a voluntary donor, those you help, or give helping hand – it is better to share your energy from the excess you have, but not from the last reserve. To do this, we must be highly organized individuals, knowing what motivates us, what kind of energy we have in full, what we can give another person is to serve the purpose, that he recovered in the shortest time. Just putting yourself in balance, we can help the people around us, to share our power, kindness, love and energy, while constantly renewing our energy resources.

FACTORS FOR A RENEWAL OF ENERGY

The factors that allow a person to renew energy. Love - is the energy of life
- Nikola Tesla (1856-1943), the inventor in the field of electrical engineering and radio engineering, engineer, physicist

If we are motivated by love, bright thoughts and pure motives, the level of our energy will always be high. Scientists have proved that through our thoughts, there is a transition from the invisible into the visible. For his work in 1981, a leading neurophysiologist Roger Sperry, together with David H. Hubel and Torsten Wiesel received the Nobel Prize [35]. That is, our thoughts have tremendous energy force. So do not neglect this factor. Even the Bible says that man thinks in his heart, so is he. And Robert Collier (1885-1950), American author, motivator and self-help specialist, says: "Any thoughts that pass through the subconscious often enough and convincingly enough, is eventually accepted." That is what a man cultivates in his mind, how he thinks, at the end becomes a reality, even if he does not want it. So think positive, do not let your mind be "contaminated" by negativism, envy, self-pity, anger, hatred or resentment. After all, it deprives us of energy and triggers disease, poverty, strife, and disasters.

1. Good nutrition and proper drinking regime.

2. The composition of the food shall be determined by the climate in which you are, special attention should be paid to the ease of cooking and the quantity of it that you eat per time. Fresh food is recommended. Cooled, heated, sour and salty foods should be avoided. Ghee is very useful. Proper nutrition – important also, is a thorough chewing of food. Do not blindly follow the modern diet, the main thing - naturalness, simplicity and a sense of intuition. The total amount of clean water to drink throughout the day should be 1.5 - 2 liters. It is necessary to drink quietly and in small sips and always in the morning on an empty stomach.

3. Breathing exercises.

4. It is necessary to learn to breathe correctly. The most effective oxygen exchange takes place in the lower part of the lung. To penetrate the air here,

it is necessary to breathe deeply - diaphragmatic breathing (breath - stomach "inflated" slowly exhale faster - the abdomen retracted, pushing the remains of recycled air).

5.   Sufficient physical activity.

6.   To keep fit and in good condition, you need to systematically engage in exercises for maintaining a healthy body. It can be a variety of exercises aimed at different groups of muscles. Also very useful going for more walks in the fresh air, jogging and walking trails.

7.   To the best of a variety of positive emotional experience.

8.   These are emotions that are aimed at creation of man from within, they fill us with warmth, strength, love and beauty, namely: joy, pleasure, elation, enthusiasm, confidence, affection, appreciation, admiration, respect, gratitude, trust. In this case, a man fills himself with the power of positive impressions, the power of love and joy. He can share with others his feelings and experiences, so that the energy will be converted, and updated both in the man and in the people with whom he is surrounded.

9.   Solitude, relaxation at one with nature, prayer.

10. This fills us with not just energy, but high-quality energy, a higher level, therefore, you need to devote time to the spiritual formation of yourself as a person. Such a person will spend time in prayer and fasting, he will know his inner man, studying spiritual literatures, he will

appreciate all that is created in this world that is nature, appreciate his relationship with his creator and the people surrounding him.

11. Get enough sleep.

12. To live fully, to work, you need to fully relax. The main form of recreation for everyone is a dream. It is during sleep you restore energy reserves of the nervous system and all functions of the human body. There is full recovery of physical and psychological functions. A refreshing, soothing, healing sleep - one of the main components of energy and human health. In the long absence of normal sleep, is often a decrease in the body's immune system, which significantly increases the risk of many diseases. The person becomes more vulnerable to a variety of viruses, infections. Reduced stress, depression may develop.

13. Conformity of inner spiritual aspirations, life purpose execution.

14. The man who found the main values of life, lives, fulfilling purpose, and every action serves humanity - in fact, is the happiest man in the world. His energy source is updated every day. He lives the mission, which is to create something great for the good of mankind. Such a person will always be full of enthusiasm, power and energy, because of giving a person gets back in abundance. So, a person who is love, goodness and joy to others, will have more and receive more.

15. Establishing good relations with people, the ability to make and maintain relationships- it is also a source of energy, especially if you're familiar with the law of respect. For any knowledge can be turned into an exchange of goods or services. Thus, high-quality energy sharing, be aware of its value and importance in the world, you get the response of energy back, but in the form of the product. If you, on the contrary, do the unwise and will ignore the value of a person, you also will get the answer to the energy of destruction, dejection and rejection, which will not be useful to you. It is worth thinking about the fact that we are the people of - love, goodness, faith, charity, and compassion, or the opposite - hatred, jealousy, betrayal and destruction.

FACTORS RESPONSIBLE FOR LOSS OF ENERGY

THE HIGHER THE ENERGY, THE BRIGHTER AND MORE FULFILLING THE PERSON'S LIFE, THE STRONGER HIS HEALTH AND THE GREATER THE POTENTIAL TO REVEAL THE GOOD HUMAN BEING.

In order to learn not to expend our energy unnecessarily and uncontrollably, it is necessary to pay attention to how you can avoid its loss.

1. Lack of physical activity. If a person is not engaged in sports or he is engaged, but not regularly, prefer travel by truck rather than to walk in the evening or go for a jog, his energy is

low. Such people are distinguished by inactivity, laziness and lack of initiative.

2. Improper diet, including fast food, excessive consumption of fatty foods and sweets. To avoid energy losses is necessary to carefully monitor the expiration date of products, as well as the presence of preservatives, stabilizers, flavor enhancers and various chemical additives.

3. Dirty air and incorrect breathing. People living in urban areas, do not breathe the cleanest air. Various plants, industrial plants, motor vehicles, which are on the roads every year release more and more waste products that adversely affect the quality of the air we breathe. This has a negative impact on our health, worsening metabolic processes in our body. Ignorance of the basic skills of proper breathing leads to a deterioration of health and loss of strength and energy.

4. Uncontrolled negative emotions (anger, fear, sadness, etc.). If a person has not learned to manage his feelings and emotions, has not learned to control himself, it is easy to fall victim to any relationship, when almost anyone can drain vitality out of him, thus depriving him of the much-needed energy to himself.

5. The mental, physical or psychological overload arising from the human inability to distribute their strength and energy, it is reasonable to organize your day, all your life. When a person puts his business on him, he begins to live in the mode of work involving all hands, forcing

him to work the body in unbalanced mode. Inability and prudent to build his live, occasionally puts a man in the face of time of unresolved issues, which also lead to the loss of energy and strength.

6.   The concern arises when we live and take care of those things that either do not happen ever, ever invented by us. If we do not learn to take a sober look at things, see the illusory nature of our fears and feelings, the anxiety will continue to drain and sap our last force, denying us any kind of energy that is present.

7.   The empty chatter. A huge amount of energy is lost due to human guff, which is not intended to provide specific assistance to another person in the creation of himself as an individual, and is just an excuse to attract attention. This indicates a lack of integrity in us, the immaturity of our personality and that needs approval from others. This will give some of them the opportunity to manipulate you, depriving you of scarce energy resources.

8.   Excessive activity (restlessness) dissipates energy and is a sign of a low energy level. These people seem to be constantly busy with something, but the best of their activities is very small. The fact that they were busy from morning till night, is the main argument in their defense. In the absence of the results, for some reason, they do not pay attention. These people do not want to think about their planning and forecasting consequences. The energy of such a person will

go nowhere, will not even understand why.

9. Bad habits. This refers to such dependent on alcohol, drugs, smoking. When a person is in a state of alcohol or drugs, he cannot control his actions, he will not be able to govern himself. Such people often are "looking for adventure", climbs into fights, splashing all their strength and energy. In an uncontrolled state, a man inflicts a lot of damages and destroys himself, draining his strength and energy.

10. Excessive or perverted sexual activity. Not understanding the purpose and value of sexual relations between husband and wife, a man can have sexual relations before marriage or outside it, to practice sexual corruption (homosexuality, lesbianism, pedophilia, masturbation and many others). These actions drain human energy, destroy it from within.

11. The artificial stimulation of the senses. Actions aimed at artificial adrenaline rush - taking part in gambling, watching horror movies, films, erotic and pornographic content, visualization when reading the literature of this kind also deplete human vitality.

12. The low level of spirituality and humanity, separation from the divine harmony and nature. The man who lives life in the world of technology and the hectic, often forgets about the higher values of life, that it was created by the Creator. Such people often live the present day, full of problems and bustle, so hardened with time. The lack of spirituality leads to the fact that a

person comes to a standstill, and sees no way out in life, ceasing to appreciate life itself. The lack of goals in life, ignorance of the issues for which he was created, leads a person, eventually, to the fact that its energy is consumed to meet the lower demand, which leads to the degradation and depletion of vitality.

So, it is very important to live in harmony with ourselves and nature, it will help maintain harmonious, full strength and energy, relations with people, no matter what plan they have. Encouragement which bring joy to the relationship will strengthen and maintain your vitality and energy levels. And if it so happens that you will encounter opposition and rejection, with the proviso of inner harmony and the ability to replenish your energy, you will be able to successfully resist all attacks and to continue to develop constructive relations, maintaining inner peace and tranquility.

So, the book is called "DISCOVER YOUR SOURCE OF LATENT ENERGY" came to an end. What we have reviewed with you, dear reader, is a very important question about the sources of our latent energy and how to use our existing energy. Latent energy - that's what is originally deposited in us by the Creator. Latent energy - that's what motivates us to always look for something new, provoking us to reach for new heights and motivates us for new adventures and discoveries. Expanding the hidden energy, we will always look for methods and ways to improve the atmosphere in everything, and even in the family. Whatever we do in life, should enhance the improvement of things, they should not be the same as they were before. Thanks to the creative beginning in us, everything must become better and more perfect. That is, we are to experience advancement in life as we tap into the power of the force of our discovered hidden energy.

Latent energy - that's what will help us to become a great, successful and influential. It's not enough to know the laws of success, the principles and prescriptions that can increase your efficiency. It is equally important the need to practice these principles in your life. There is a stunning example of how one woman, having learned of the presence of latent energy in her, and how to tap into this energy, started to apply this knowledge to her life. She saw in the villages that some many women were dependent on alcohol. Because of this, there was suffering in the families and children were neglected, as a consequence of their lifestyle, these women were deprived of their parental rights by sending their children to boarding schools. To help these families get out of the difficult situation, she established with like-minded people, a centre for parents and children from such families, where they could spend more time together, teaching them to create and build something valuable and useful, rather than to destroy themselves and create some societal problems. Through such activities, the woman I'm talking about has the ability to give attention, love, and good to people in need of the support. She truly filled herself with energy, living according to the laws of love and passing it around. The nature of the Creator - a love that is always thinking about how to please and serve the other people. Do not let self-centeredness steal away your energy!

THE GOLDEN NUGGETS

- The higher the energy level, the brighter and full of human life, the stronger his health and the greater the potential is able to reveal in the man
- In order not to expend your energy unnecessarily and uncontrollably, it is necessary to pay attention to how you can avoid its loss
- If we are motivated by love, bright thoughts and pure motives, the level of our energy will always be high
- The renewal the energy resources of human depend on the following factors
  - › Good nutrition and proper drinking regime.
  - › Breathing exercises.
  - › Adequate physical activity.
  - › To the best variety of positive emotional experience.
  - › Privacy, relaxation, being at one with nature, prayer
  - › Get enough sleep.
  - › Compliance Activities inner spiritual aspirations, life purpose execution.
- Factors that causes energy loss:
  - › Lack of physical activity
  - › Malnutrition
  - › Dirty air and incorrect breathing practice
  - › Uncontrolled negative emotions

- Mental, physical or psychological overload
- Anxiety
- Guff
- Excessive activity (restlessness), bad habits
- Excessive or perverted sexual activity
- Artificial stimulation of the senses
- Low level of spirituality and humanity, separation from the divine harmony of nature

SELF-EXAMINATION TEST

It should be noted only one answer is necessary for each question or statement. Next to each answer are marked point. Stacked score will determine the outcome of your training.

1. How do you intend not to spend your energy unnecessarily and uncontrollably?

a. I do what I want - eat whatever I want, drink, drugs, smoke, swear and in every way I can to provoke other people to aggression and irritation. And my behavior has no effect on the strength of my vital energy, and in some cases even on the contrary, it increases the energy in me - **1 point**

b. I often spend time outdoors, play sports and watch the quality of food I eat, try to be in harmony with myself and others, cultivate a higher spiritual qualities of my person. I try to help everyone who needs my help - **4 points**

c. In order not to unnecessarily expend my energy, I do sports, adhere to proper nutrition, healthy foods, try not to get irritated and control my emotions - **3 points**

d. None of my actions can affect the quantity and quality of my life energy - **2 points**

2. My energy can be compensated for, through such factors as:

a. Fully concentrate on myself, fulfilling all the desires and needs for a permanent vacation, comfort, elimination of any kind of activity - **2 points**

b. My energy is impossible to fill, I am more and more devastated and depleted every day, I hate the world and all that is in it, and that nothing can help me – **1 point**

c. To compensate for my energy, I take care of myself, of my feelings, I deviate not to the right and left, I am "here and now", taking care of my integrity - **3 points**

d. Solitude, prayer, caring both about my appearance, physical body, emotions, intellect (constantly educating myself), and the inner man. I fill the higher the energy of love, joy and patience and help others to develop their qualitative skills and replenish their energy - **4 points**

3. What is your state of health of your physical body at the moment?

a. I feel completely overwhelmed. The only thing that helps me stay in shape and feel good - it's alcohol, hookah, various energy drinks and stabilizers - **1 point**

b. No matter the situation that confronts my life, it does not prevent me to lead an active and healthy lifestyle. I do not only take care of my own health, but also the health of people who need my help - **4 points**

c. I feel good at this hour. I actively go in for sports, eat healthy food, watch out for my body hygiene - **3 points**

d. Physically my condition is more or less stable. I do not strain myself at work, almost never do sports, do not follow a healthy diet - **2 points**

4. How do you communicate and show emotions?

a. When communicating I often watch over what I say, and to whom I speak. I'm afraid to offend the person with whom I communicate or look in his eyes, silly. my emotions do not show, but am always constantly internally tensed - **2 points**

b. I talk like everyone else. I always say what I think and do not hesitate the use of strong language to more clearly paint the picture. Regarding emotions, I often do not hold back. And how can I restrain or control them? I can get angry, I get irritated, often defend my point of view, because I'm always righ - **1 point**

c. Generally, in communion with other people I am sincere and open. I find it easy to communicate, because I see close friend in every person. I'm emotionally open person, I do not hesitate to

show emotions and know how to control them
- **3 points**

d. For me to communicate with people - it is very opportunity to give peace, happiness, goodness and love another person. I am open and always ready to listen and help. I show those emotions that can build and develop others. I am able to fully control my feelings and emotions - **4 points**

5. Will you develop your intellectual capacity?

a. What should I develop? I have, and so I know everything! I attend seminars and trainings at work to grow the career ladder - **2 points**

b. I do not develop the intellectual sphere, because I do not see the point in it. I am satisfied with myself and the way I live, and this is good enough for me. Study hard? I do not like to study. I prefer to live in comfort - **1 point**

c. I do from time to time engaged in the development of my intellectual level. I read educational books, watch TV, go deep in knowledge in areas that are important to me - **3 points**

d. I try to fully develop. The intellectual sphere is very important in a full and quality life of my person. I'm everywhere and everything, and allow the further use of knowledge to achieve the objectives in the development and perfection of the world - **4 points.**

TEST RESULTS

From 0 to 7 points - This score indicates that you do not see the resources in your life. You constantly have live in short supply of energy. You feel squeezed like a lemon and do not know what to do with it. Ignorance and the inability to use a backup power in your life leads to the fact that you are often irritated and tear on others. Close People rarely see you full of vitality. This book is not by chance in your hands. It will help you learn how to properly use your energy, be prudent and focused. Going forward, in spite of everything, and to open a new sources of stored energy.

From 8 to 16 points - this score suggests that you do not just wonder about your identity and integrity, you also care about the correct functioning of organs and systems, as well as the movement of energy in your body. Do you care about your health and that of friends and relatives? Do you have knowledge of the principles of many acquisitions and increase of quality of energy within yourself? For your full growth and development, you need the knowledge to help people in need. Also, you would do well to learn to always go forward and achieve the goals ahead of you. Believe in yourself, in the value of your life to this world. Learn to not only reserve for yourself, but also to give to others. After all, in the universal law of sowing and reaping. The more you give, the more you gain.

From 16 to 20 points - this number of points indicates that you consciously live every day of your life to the full. You know how to manage the internal processes of your body. In your daily life, you are using energy efficiently and wisely. You are able to find (to discover) all new sources of inner vitality. Nothing can stop you, as you already do not live for yourself but through you, the world has become more beautiful, better, more perfect, more beautiful. You are a unique person! You are never alone, your life's value keeps on increasing, because it is filled with life and love lives of others.

PRACTICAL TASKS

1. Where did you lose energy the most? Make a list of actions that are normal in daily life which lead to rash and a waste of your energy. Develop an algorithm of actions, which will allow you to avoid this in the future.

2. Write down the list of mechanisms to replenish your energy. Make a plan of action in everyday life, which will help you to be full of strength and energy.

EPILOGUE

So, are at the tail end of this book, "discover your source of latent energy!". On its pages, we found that the energy is not lost, it just changes from one form to another. What does this mean for us? At first, …

Do not agree with the fact that you have something that does not work

Before you give up, remember why you started.

- Author Unknown

There should not be such a thing, that there is something you do not know 'how' or 'cannot'. EVERYONE CAN MAKE HIMSELF TO BECOME, WHAT HE WANTS TO SEE HIMELF BE. You can make yourself successful, beautiful, skinny, pumped, i.e. exactly the way you want to be, how you present yourself in your wildest dreams. And it's all available to you through labor: physical, mental, intellectual, spiritual, and so on..

You need to:

- detect the latent energy
- start to release it through labor
- guide it in the right direction to the designated time to receive the expected result

I want to remind you, dear reader, a certain wisdom that **victory always comes one step away from defeat.** Remember: NO LOSERS IN LIFE! Therefore, we cannot agree that there is something you do not have. As long as we breathe, while our heart is beating in our chest, we can fight and we can change everything. As long as we are alive, we can continue to make the next attempt.

Because all you need you already have: You already have all you need, strength and energy, to take your place in life, to get all of what you just want. Even if today you are a loser, it does not mean that the more you try, nothing ever happens, you cannot change yourself. You already have the most important tool to change yourself and your place in life - it is work. Starting to use it, you will discover all you need to succeed.

Secondly...

You do not have to stay there, where the fate of life abandoned you.

The fact that a person was born in a stable does not make him a horse.

- The Duke of Wellington (1769-1852), a well-known military and political leader of Irish descent

YOU SHOULD NEVER REGRET WHAT HAD ALREADY PASSED.

Usually, if we fail, make a mistake, you start to regret it and to be engaged in self-flagellation, "Oh! I did bad, I did wrong! ". We begin to live in the past, whereas this cannot be done, because that behavior does nothing good. So, what should be dealt with - it is right now, being where you were, to begin to do what needs to be done. You need to understand for yourself that you have not lost anything, you just used your existing energy turned into some useless, unwanted, problematic things. So, the energy has not disappeared anywhere, you have it, you just need to work hard to translate it into what you want. There is no reason to regret!

One student asked the teacher:

- What is the best time to plant a tree?

The sage replied:

- This time it was twenty years ago. But if you do not put it 20 years ago, then the best time - to put it is now.

Never too late to start, while you are alive. You have not lost anything. Do not engage in self-pity! **You just need to start doing now, how it should be really.**

Do what you can, with what you have, where you are

- Theodore Roosevelt.

We all need to start releasing the energy that we have. Do not waste energy, not to regret the unfinished projects and unfulfilled plans. So the recipe is simple: you need to act!

Lesions are common, all the people from time to time fail, but that should not stop us on our way. Any loss and any failure should be a stepping stone or a springboard for the next takeoff. In any case, we have to try again and to continue to make an attempt, without giving up until then, until you get it. "The man who is not inclined to fight for what he wants, is not worthy of what he wants" - wisely said Frederic Beigbeder (1965), modern French novelist, essayist, literary critic and editor. Therefore, the only way not to stay there, where you rescind to a life or fate - is to fight as long as you do not get that to which you aspire.

If what you are working on is:
- intellectually
- spiritually
- physically,

then you will be able to destroy all the poverty and misery in your life, you will be able to release your full potential and live a full and eventful life!

Even failures can draw energy

I personally love my mistakes as much as successes. Because they show the border, for which cannot be crossed.

**- Mikhail Prokhorov (1965),
Russian politician and
businessman, billionaire**

We must learn to see the value of our errors, miscalculations and blunders. Even successful people as billionaires, see themselves in more pluses than minuses. So why not adopt their approach to life?

- *«Failures - a great way to get rid of everything unnecessary,"* - says JK Rowling, the author of novels about Harry Potter. She was left with a small child in her arms, she worked as a waitress and lived on welfare at the time when she started to write her first book in this series. This woman did not spend her life and energy on bronzer. She converted her not very pleasant circumstances into creativity - the realization of the dreams, that lived in her heart. Thanks to the embedded labor, JK Rowling has become one of the most popular authors in the history of mankind. Although her book was originally rejected by dozens of publishers, in the end, it was published only because, the director of the publishing house was persuaded by his eight-year old daughter.

- *«he missed more than 9000 times in his career."* *I've lost almost 300 games.* I'm 26 again trusted to make the decisive shot, which could bring my team a win, and I missed. I suffered a lot of losses in my life. And because of this, I succeeded, "- the words of Michael Jordan, which we have already mentioned in this book. He says that his success owed to failures and blunders. Sports Legend, which is considered one of the best players in basketball history, also passed through a crisis in his life when his career was just beginning, he could not even make the school team. [35]

- Star James Carville came to the limelight during Bill Clinton's 1992 presidential campaign, when he became his assistant. Today he is considered one of the best of the current generation of politicians' establishment. But before he got a job at 40 years, he was deeply grounded: without a penny in his pocket, and without the proper experience. He could not even get a credit card with the bank. In the eyes of all he looked like an absolute failure. But due to the fact that James Carville didn't give up in the end, he was in the White House, and gained such position and status that surprised many of those who knew him before [37]. The man was able to detect a stored energy source and open them, for the benefit of himself and all others. He refused to stay there, where fate left him, and because of that, his name is now ringing in the ears of everyone.

- *« Thank God, Beethoven can write music, because the more he did not know how."* Perhaps the ability to write music - and it was only the talent of this genius, but it was enough to discover in it a source of energy for his life and work, which have allowed the great German step into eternity. He has long been dead, but the great music of Beethoven sounds is reminding us that we must live in order that we can survive in the centuries that will allow us to leave our mark in history. Beethoven's path had not been easy: like most people on this earth, he had experienced the frustration, ups and downs. But he did not let the circumstances lead him to give up and surrender. He never allowed himself to think that he will not turn and, in the end, he got much more than he expected from himself or the people around. His early talent for music and the violin got no one impressed, and teachers felt that it was hopeless. Therefore, the formation of Ludwig took his father, who could see the potential in his son. Although eventually Beethoven lost his hearing, the disease did not stop him, and four of the greatest works were written by him when he was completely deaf. [38]

- *«In the morning, I need twenty minutes, to cry, to come to terms with the fact that I had lost, and in the end, to say to myself: and now - ahead."* These words belong to Christopher Reeve (1952-2004), an actor who was fortunate to play Superman, but was not lucky enough to fall off the horse, as he was paralyzed. Today you are "a horse", and are the focus of a wide range of public, and tomorrow your position may change by 180 degrees: you can be sick, paralyzed, useless and thrown overboard. If you were inspired when you played the role of Superman, why not find ways to draw energy to live and when everything has changed beyond recognition? Cry in the morning, Christopher Reeve went on to live a lot of traveling and speaking on behalf of people suffering injuries of the spine, raising funds for charities and even became a director. He learned to be content with what he had, and use it to help others. [39]

- *«I have never considered myself a poor girl from the ghetto, which was able to achieve something. I consider myself a person who from an early age who knew that she herself is responsible for her life and must achieve something",* - says of herself Oprah Winfrey (1954), American tele-vision host, actress, producer, social activist, leading current -Show "The Oprah Winfrey Show." Almost everyone knows the story of her life, she had a terrible childhood, in which there has been violence and extreme poverty. Did this woman stay where fate had put her? No, she did everything possible to open her stored energy source and became a successful person. [40]

- *"I know that I can make mistakes, but it does not save me from being able to still make them. I get up only when I fall ",* - said Vincent van Gogh (1853-1890), Dutch painter postimpressionist. The artist suffered from manic-depressive psychosis, so most of the time he could barely function. Recognition for his life, he did not wait, so that, by our standards, it did not become a successful person. But today his work is considered one of the greatest works of art. He found the strength to live and continue to do, in spite of everything. There were many things that could have stopped him and let him - just like all of us. But he found more and more of his energy sources, so that today we can admit that he has been successful: his work has survived him, and remained for centuries [41].

As often as it happens: the man tried to do something once, twice, thrice - has not turned out, and given up! But to see the fulfillment of your dreams, you need to fight for it. To achieve this goal, we will have to give our maximum effort and resources - "give everything" for one hundred percent. Success will not be cheap! And it all starts with an intense mental work, you will find the strength to discover and tap into YOUR SOURCE OF LATENT ENERGY.

REFERENCES:

1. Dergach I. "How to live with his mind. Completely paralyzed man has become one of the best administrators in the country. " Source: Not invalid.ru -

2. Sherstuk O. "Blind artist paints a touch." Source: Not invalid.ru

3. N. Vujcic "Life without limits. The path to the amazing happy life "

4. "Miles Hilton-Barber" Source: Lyudi.ru

5. "The law of conservation of energy." Wikipedia -

6. "The law of conservation of energy." Dictionaries and encyclopedias and Akademik - Tikhonov "Transformation of energy in chloroplasts - the organelles of a plant cell energy conversion", 1996

7. "Henry Ford - a success story, biography, quotes." Blog Kozhin. R. - http://www.myrouble.ru/genri-ford-istoriya-uspexa/

8. M. Gladwell "Geniuses and outsiders'

9. The population of the earth ", Wikipedia - ru.wikipedia.org/wiki/Население_Земли

10. Maslow's hierarchy of needs. Wikipedia - https://ru.wikipedia.org/wiki/Абрахам Maslow

11. Table of living standards around the world in 2013 - http://gotoroad.ru/best/indexlife

12. "Benjamin Franklin" Wikipedia - https://ru.wikipedia.org/wiki/Франклин_Бенджамин

13. "George Washington Carver," Wikipedia - https://ru.wikipedia.org/wiki/%D0%9A%D0%B0%D1%80%D0%B2%D0%B5%D1%80,_%D0 % 94% D0% B6% D0% BE% D1% 80% D0% B4% D0% B6_% D0% 92% D0%

B0% D1% 88% D0% B8% D0% BD% D0% B3% D1% 82 % D0% BE% D0% BD

14. "The habits of great writers» - http://pikabu.ru/story/privyichki_velikikh_pisateley_1047996

15. "Creative writing routine» - http://theoryand-practice.ru/posts/7100-pisatelskaya-rutina-syuzen-zon-tag-dzhek-keruak-i-mark-tven-o-rabochikh-ritualakh

16. Templeton D. "D. Templeton 90 minutes. World laws of life "

17. "Savants: Patients genius» -https: //www.drive2.ru/b/288230376151944216/

18. "savant syndrome - a special case of autism» - http://www.psyworld.ru/for-adults/kaleido-scope/102-2008-08-20-13-57-17.html

19. "savant syndrome: a man became a mathematics genius after brain injury", 7 May 2014 - http://www.infoniac.ru/news/Sindrom-savanta-muzhchina-stal-ge-niem-matematiki-posle-travmy-mozga. html

20. "Thomas Alva Edison". Source: Wikipedia - http://ru.wikipedia.org/wiki/%D0%AD%D0%B4%D0%B8%D1%81%D0%BE%D0%BD,_%D0%A2%D0%BE % D0% BC% D0% B0% D1% 81_% D0% 90% D0% BB% D0% B2% D0% B0

21. Dictionary of Business Terms. Akademik.ru. 2001

22. "The concept and theoretical basis of handwriting." Kriminalistka - http://elosoft.ru/ponjtie_i_teoretich-eskie_osnovy_pocherkovedenie-2.php

23. "How to become a millionaire. Newspaper "abroad" № 6 (215) -http:? //www.zagran.kiev.ua/article.php New = 215 & idart = 21517

24. Ephraim TF New Dictionary of Russian language. Explanatory-derivation. - M .: Russian language, 2000

25. "Sex and boxing! Myths and Reality. " Boxing News from Alexander Kolesnikov - http://akboxing. ru/2013/02/04/52353.html

26. K. Sultanov "Can sex before the game negatively affect athletic achievements?» - Http://www.geo.ru/ futbolu-ne-pomekha

27. http://olgarazmazova.jimdo.com/

28. "How to find free time!» - Http://www.nelevex. com/2012/05/01/kak-najti-svobodnoe-vremya/

29. "Why AmericanAirlines airline with a single olive saved $ 40 000?» - Http://pochemuchka.info/other/ pochemu-aviakompaniya-american-airlines-pri-po- moschi-odnoy-masliny-sekonomila-40-000-dollarov

30. PG Pererva. Art self-marketing. Employment without problems.

31. "SkazkaiElfiki» - http://www.syntone.ru/library/ article_other/content/6162.html

32. "Run hidden reserves of the body the power of thought." Source: © http: //sna-kantata.ru/zapus- kaem-skryityie-rezervyi-organizma-siloy-myisli/

33. "Michael Jordan." Wikipedia - https://ru.wikipedia. org/wiki/%D0%94%D0%B6%D0%BE%D1%80%D0%B 4%D0%B0%D0%BD,_%D0%9C%D0 % B0% D0% B9% D0% BA% D0% BB

34. "9 stories about success, born out of failure." Project: 5 areas - http://5sfer.com/11381-9-istorij-ob-us- pexe-rodivshemsya-iz-neudach.html

35. "Ludwig Beethoven baths" Wikipedia - http:// ru.wikipedia.org/wiki/%D0%91%D0%B5%D1%82%D1 %85%D0%BE%D0%B2%D0%B5 % D0% BD, _% D0% 9B% D1% 8E% D0% B4% D0% B2% D0% B8% D0% B3_% D0% B2% D0% B0% D0% BD

36. "Christopher Reeve" Wikipedia - https://ru.wiki-pedia.org/wiki/%D0%A0%D0%B8%D0%B2,_%D0%9A%D1%80%D0%B8%D1% 81% D1% 82% D0% BE% D1% 84% D0% B5% D1% 80

37. "OpraUinfri" Wikipedia - https://ru.wiki-pedia.org/wiki/%D0%A3%D0%B8%D0%B-D%D1%84%D1%80%D0%B8,_%D0%9E % D0% BF% D1% 80% D0% B0

38. "Vincent Van Gogh", Wikipedia - https://ru.wikipedia.org/wiki/%D0%92%D0%B0%D0%B-D_%D0%93%D0%BE%D0%B3,_%D0 % 92% D0% B8% D0% BD% D1% 81% D0% B5% D0% BD% D1% 82

SUNDAY ADELAJA'S
BIOGRAPHY

Pastor Sunday Adelaja is the Founder and Senior Pastor of The Embassy of the Blessed Kingdom of God for All Nations Church in Kyiv, Ukraine.

Sunday Adelaja is a Nigerian-born Leader, Thinker, Philosopher, Transformation Strategist, Pastor, Author and Innovator who lives in Kiev, Ukraine.

At 19, he won a scholarship to study in the former Soviet Union. He completed his master's program in Belorussia State University with distinction in journalism.

At 33, he had built the largest evangelical church in Europe — The Embassy of the Blessed Kingdom of God for All Nations.

Sunday Adelaja is one of the few individuals in our world who has been privileged to speak in the United Nations, Israeli Parliament, Japanese Parliament and the United States Senate.

The movement he pioneered has been instrumental in reshaping lives of people in the Ukraine, Russia and about 50 other nations where he has his branches.

His congregation, which consists of ninety-nine percent white Europeans, is a cross-cultural model of the church for the 21st century.

His life mission is to advance the Kingdom of God on earth by raising a generation of history mak-

ers who will live for a cause larger, bigger and greater than themselves. Those who will live like Jesus and transform every sphere of the society in every nation as a model of the Kingdom of God on earth.

His economic empowerment program has succeeded in raising over 200 millionaires in the short period of three years.

Sunday Adelaja is the author of over 300 books, many of which are translated into several languages including Russian, English, French, Chinese, German, etc.

His work has been widely reported by world media outlets such as The Washington Post, The Wall Street Journal, New York Times, Forbes, Associated Press, Reuters, CNN, BBC, German, Dutch and French national television stations.

Pastor Sunday is happily married to his "Princess" Bose Dere-Adelaja. They are blessed with three children: Perez, Zoe and Pearl.

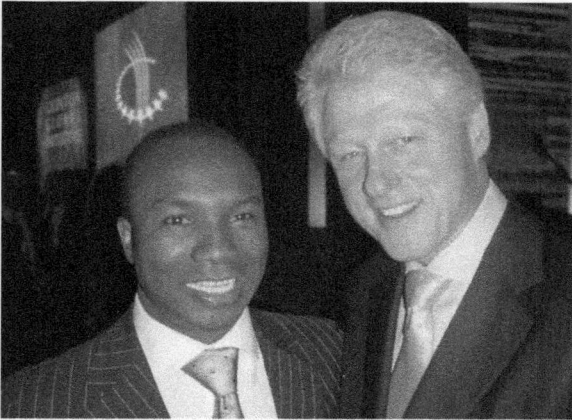

Bill Clinton —
42Nd President Of The
United States (1993–2001),
Former Arcansas State
Governor

Ariel "Arik" Sharon —
Israeli Politician, Israeli
Prime Minister (2001–2006)

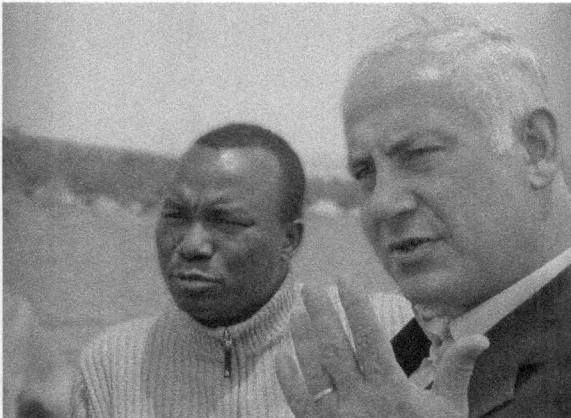

Benjamin Netanyahu —
Statesman Of Israel. Israeli
Prime Minister (1996–1999),
Acting Prime Minister
(From 2009)

Jean ChrEtien —
Canadian Politician,
20ᵀʰ Prime Minister Of
Canada, Minister Of Justice
Of Canada, Head Of Liberan
Party Of Canada

Rudolph Giuliani —
American Political Actor,
Mayor Of New York Served
From 1994 To 2001. Actor
Of Republican Party

Colin Powell —
Is An American Statesman
And A Retired Four-Star
General In The Us Army,
65ᵀʰ United States Secretary
Of State

Peter J. Daniels —
Is A Well-Known And
Respected Australian
Christian International
Business Statesman Of
Substance

Madeleine
Korbel Albright —
An American Politician And
Diplomat, 64[Th] United States
Secretary Of State

Kenneth Robert
Livingstone —
An English Politician,
1[St] Mayor Of London
(4 May 2000 – 4 May
2008), Labour Party
Representative

Sir Richard Charles Nicholas Branson —
English Business Magnate, Investor And Philanthropist. He Founded The *Virgin Group*, Which Controls More Than 400 Companies

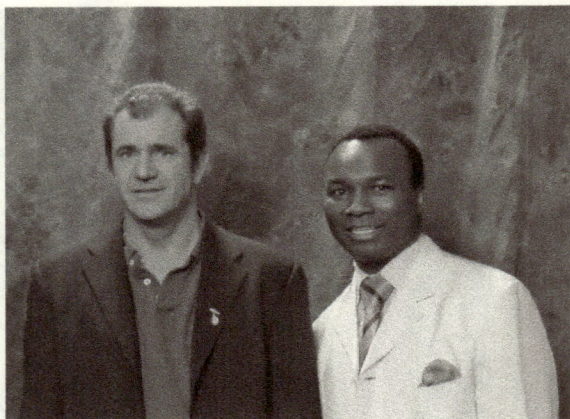

Mel Gibson —
American Actor And Filmmaker

Chuck Norris —
American Martial Artist, Actor, Film Producer And Screenwriter

Christopher Tucker —
American Actor
And Comedian

Bernice Albertine King —
American Minister Best
Known As The Youngest
Child Of Civil Rights Leaders
Martin Luther King Jr. And
Coretta Scott King Andrew

Andrew Young — American
Politician, Diplomat, And
Activist, 14Th United States
Ambassador To The United
Nations, 55Th Mayor Of
Atlanta

General Wesley Kanne Clark — 4-Star General And Nato Supreme Allied Commander

Dr. Sunday Adelaja's family:
Perez, Pearl, Zoe and Pastor Bose Adelaja

FOLLOW
SUNDAY ADELAJA
ON SOCIAL MEDIA

Subscribe And Read Pastor Sunday's Blog:
www.sundayadelajablog.com
Follow these links and listen to over 200
of Pastor Sunday`s Messages free of charge:
http://sundayadelajablog.com/content/
Follow Pastor Sunday on Twitter:
www.twitter.com/official_pastor

Join Pastor Sunday's Facebook page to stay in touch:
www.facebook.com/pastor.
sunday.adelaja
Visit our websites for more
information about Pastor
Sunday's ministry:
http://www.godembassy.com
http://www.pastorsunday.com
http://sundayadelaja.de

CONTACT

FOR DISTRIBUTION OR TO ORDER
BULK COPIES OF THIS BOOK,
PLEASE CONTACT US:

USA

CORNERSTONE PUBLISHING

info@thecornerstonepublishers.com

+1 (516) 547-4999

www.thecornerstonepublishers.com

AFRICA

SUNDAY ADELAJA MEDIA LTD.

E-mail: btawolana@hotmail.com

+2348187518530, +2348097721451, +2348034093699

LONDON, UK

PASTOR ABRAHAM GREAT

abrahamagreat@gmail.com

+447711399828, +441908538141

KIEV, UKRAINE

pa@godembassy.org

Mobile: +380674401958

BEST
SELLING
AUTHOR

Best Selling Books by Dr. Sunday Adelaja
Available on Amazon.com and Okadabooks.com

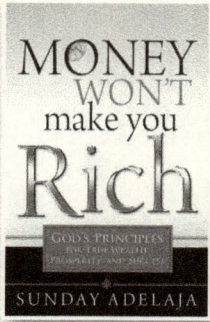

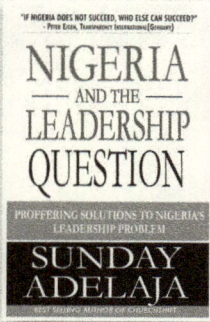

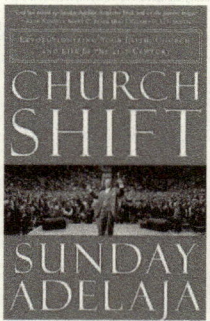

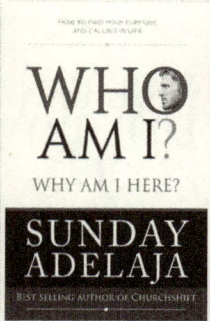

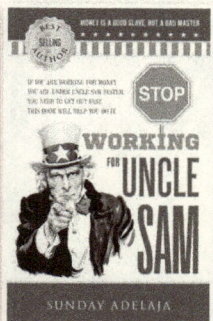

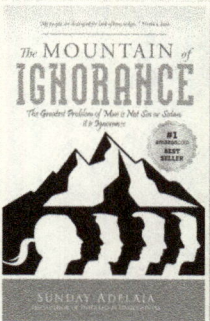

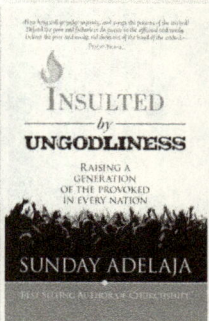

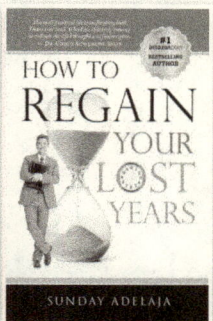

MONEY WON'T make you Rich
GOD'S PRINCIPLES FOR TRUE WEALTH, PROSPERITY AND SUCCESS
SUNDAY ADELAJA

NIGERIA AND THE LEADERSHIP QUESTION
"IF NIGERIA DOES NOT SUCCEED, WHO ELSE CAN SUCCEED?"
- PETER EIGEN, TRANSPARENCY INTERNATIONAL (GERMANY)
PROFFERING SOLUTIONS TO NIGERIA'S LEADERSHIP PROBLEM
SUNDAY ADELAJA
BEST SELLING AUTHOR OF CHURCHSHIFT

MYLES MUNROE
. . . FINDING ANSWERS TO WHY GOOD PEOPLE DIE TRAGIC AND EARLY DEATHS
SUNDAY ADELAJA

THE KINGDOM DRIVEN LIFE
Thy Kingdom Come, Thy will be Done on Earth . . .
SUNDAY ADELAJA
BEST SELLING AUTHOR OF CHURCHSHIFT

CHURCH SHIFT
SUNDAY ADELAJA

WHO AM I?
WHY AM I HERE?
SUNDAY ADELAJA
BEST SELLING AUTHOR OF CHURCHSHIFT

ONLY GOD can save NIGERIA: What a Myth!
SUNDAY ADELAJA
The Author of Nigeria and the Leadership Question

STOP WORKING FOR UNCLE SAM
MONEY IS A GOOD SLAVE, BUT A BAD MASTER
BEST SELLING AUTHOR
SUNDAY ADELAJA

The MOUNTAIN of IGNORANCE
The Greatest Problem of Man is Not Sin or Satan, it is Ignorance
SUNDAY ADELAJA

OLORUNWA

INSULTED by UNGODLINESS
RAISING A GENERATION OF THE PROVOKED IN EVERY NATION
SUNDAY ADELAJA
BEST SELLING AUTHOR OF CHURCHSHIFT

HOW TO REGAIN YOUR LOST YEARS
#1 INTERNATIONAL BESTSELLING AUTHOR
SUNDAY ADELAJA

BEST SELLING BOOKS BY DR. SUNDAY ADELAJA
AVAILABLE ON AMAZON.COM AND OKADABOOKS.COM

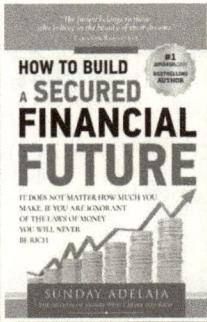

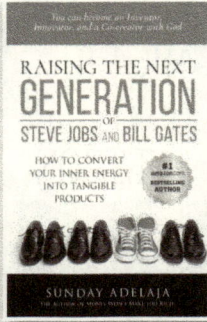

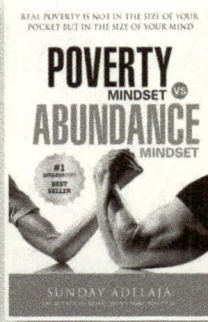

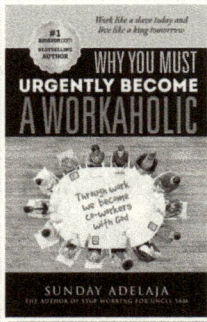

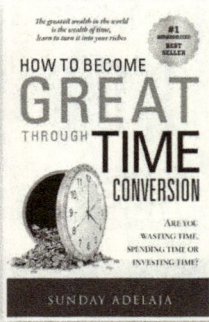

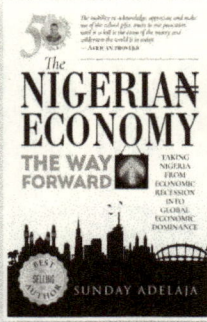

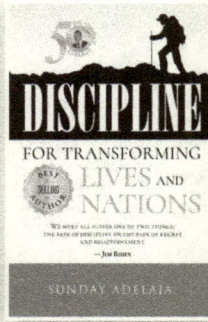

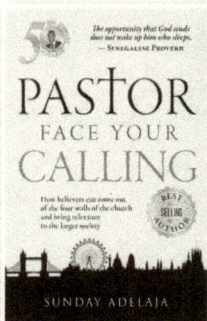

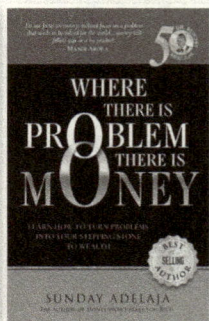

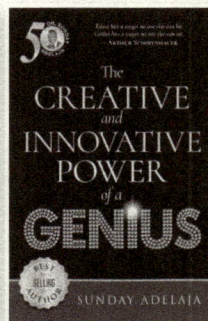

GOLDEN JUBILEE SERIES BOOKS
BY DR. SUNDAY ADELAJA

FOR DISTRIBUTION OR TO ORDER BULK COPIES OF THIS BOOKS, PLEASE CONTACT US:

USA | CORNERSTONE PUBLISHING
E-mail: info@thecornerstonepublishers.com, +1 (516) 547-4999
www.thecornerstonepublishers.com

AFRICA | SUNDAY ADELAJA MEDIA LTD.
E-mail: btawolana@hotmail.com
+2348187518530, +2348097721451, +2348034093699

LONDON, UK | PASTOR ABRAHAM GREAT
E-mail: abrahamagreat@gmail.com, +447711399828, +441908538141

KIEV, UKRAINE |
E-mail: pa@godembassy.org, Mobile: +380674401958